ALPHABET SOUP

The Essential Guide to LGBTQ2+ Inclusion at Work

MICHAEL BACH

PAGE TWO

Cataloguing in publication information is
available from Library and Archives Canada.

ISBN 978-1-77458-085-1 (print)
ISBN 978-1-77458-086-8 (ebook)

Page Two
pagetwo.com

Edited by Kendra Ward
Copyedited by Christine Lyseng Savage
Interior design by Jennifer Lum
Interior illustrations by Setareh Ashrafologhalai
Printed and bound in Canada by Friesens
Distributed in Canada by Raincoast Books
Distributed in the US and internationally by Macmillan

22 23 24 25 26   5 4 3 2 1

michaelbach.com

This book is dedicated to every nine-year-old LGBTQ2+ kid out there struggling to figure out who they are. Hopefully, it will help make a world where you can be your fabulous self and not feel any shame.

CONTENTS

OPENING THOUGHTS

No one told me when I wrote my first book, *Birds of All Feathers: Doing Diversity and Inclusion Right*, that I was going to have to write a second book. Can't I just be Internet famous now? I wrote a whole book by myself, and it even became a bestseller and won an award. Isn't that enough? Sheesh.

In writing *Birds*, I wanted to establish a level set of information for people on the topic of diversity and inclusion (D&I) broadly. Let's face it—it's a capital-B Big topic with a lot of intricacies. In this book, I'm digging deeper into the specifics of one particular demographic group under the pan-diversity umbrella to provide more detailed knowledge. So, if you haven't read *Birds* yet, you're probably going to want to read that book too.

Alphabet Soup is all about sexual orientation and gender identity and expression; the magical, mysterious world of the LGBTQ2+ communities; and how people can do a better job of creating inclusive spaces for those of us who don't fit into the box of "straight" and "cis." And don't worry if I've lost you already; I promise that by the time you've finished this book, you will understand those words and what "LGBTQ2+" means, if nothing else.

The first thing I need to explain is that the initialism LGBTQ2+ (or another set of similar letters—but more on that later) represents two different things: (1) sexual orientation and (2) gender identity and gender expression. That's right. The letters in the initialism may represent *either* sexuality or gender—or both! I always feel like I should apologize for this because I think it's probably quite confusing for people who aren't members of the LGBTQ2+ communities. So, allow me to present you with an example to explain.

Meet my friend Jenn. Jenn was born Michael (and I'm not talking about myself; there is more than one Michael in the LGBTQ2+ communities). More specifically, at birth, the doctor assigned the sex "male" to Michael. (Doctor looked down, saw penis, exclaimed, "BOY!") In the 1980s, Michael realized he wasn't like the other boys, and for him, at that moment, that meant he was gay (this was his sexual orientation). Then, in the 1990s, Michael realized that he was not gay, he was ... a she. So, Michael transitioned to her true self, as Jenn (this is her gender identity and her gender expression). She also realized that she liked girls, so she came out as a lesbian (back to her sexual orientation). Further along Jenn's journey, she realized that her sexuality was fluid, and she now identifies as queer (or, as she likes to joke, she's too old to get picky). 🌐

Sorry for blowing your mind so early in the book, but thank goodness there are emojis to explain your feelings. Remember when we just had to use words? #progress

Sexuality and gender are not the same thing, but they are interrelated... sometimes. You'll find a lot of myth-busting throughout this book. That's one of the main purposes of the book: to educate. A big barrier to creating fully inclusive spaces is plain old ignorance. There are a lot of straight, cisgender people who have the best of intentions, but we all know what the road to hell was paved with. You don't know what you don't know, and the only way you can learn is by reading my books. And *only* my books! (Okay, maybe some other books, but mine first.)

Wait... why do I keep saying "communities," instead of LGBTQ2+ "community"? Oh, sweetie. #adorable. Simply put, there isn't just *one* LGBTQ2+ community. There are *many* LGBTQ2+ communities. If we consider only the community of "sexual diversity" and the community of "gender diversity," we have two communities. Digging deeper and applying an intersectional lens (where we look at how individual characteristics overlap and influence identity as well as discrimination and privilege—which I talked about in *Birds of All Feathers*—which you've read, right?), we end up with communities within communities. We're like those adorable matryoshka dolls (aka Russian nesting dolls, for those that don't be Russian—which I just said in a cheesy Boris and Natasha accent). The LGBTQ2+ community is made up of many communities that come together under one umbrella.

Sadly, it's not all lollipops and unicorns, and there are some significant tensions and conflicts within the big rainbow world. Although I'm a gay man, I'm white and cisgender too. My life is *very* different from that of a Trans* person, or a person of color. And a Trans* person of color... well, let's just say that life is not always a picnic.[1] I'm not saying there's some weird war going on, like with the Jets and the Sharks, but it's also not perfect. Like my first marriage, it's complicated.

This book is about LGBTQ2+ inclusion in the workplace, first and foremost. That's my area of expertise, after all. But LGBTQ2+ inclusion goes well beyond workplaces, to include schools, religious and faith groups, and other community settings. If you're inclusive of LGBTQ2+ people at work, there's a pretty good chance that you'll be inclusive of your niece when they identify as gender non-binary and introduce you to their Trans* genderqueer aromantic partner. And we're back to that head-explosion emoji.

Alphabet Soup is a guide that will take you, my faithful reader, on a journey of discovery with the objective of turning you and your organization into "active allies"—a term I will explain later. Like it or not, LGBTQ2+ people need allies to help us achieve that elusive goal of true inclusion. Everything in this book can be applied to a workplace and engaging with employees, as well as interactions with volunteers, customers, students, parishioners, or just everyday people on the street.

When it comes to LGBTQ2+ inclusion at work and in communities, I'm always reminded of one of my favorite conversations. Many years ago, I was speaking with the head of HR for an organization located in a western European country that shall remain nameless to protect the guilty. She was telling me about the company's work in diversity and inclusion, with no mention of work in the LGBTQ2+ communities. When I probed, she defensively explained that they don't discuss "these things" at work. I looked over at a photo on her desk and asked if the man in it with her was her husband, to which she responded in the affirmative (it was a wedding photo, and she was wearing a white wedding dress, so chances were good). I pointed out that the photo was a statement of her sexual orientation. I likely didn't need to ask her what sexual orientation she identified with, because she had it on display. (I probably should have asked... but let's focus on the point.) That was an eye-opening moment for her.

She looked at me, puzzled, and said, "So what you're saying is we should be creating a place where David can put a picture of his partner on his desk just like I can?" (David was one of her colleagues who is gay.) She realized that I wasn't asking about sex; I was asking about sexual orientation (never mind discussing gender beyond the binary, because that was way more than she could've handled at that time, but I was taking my win). Light bulb on!

This book is also very personal. There's an entire chapter just about me, and not just because of my overinflated sense of self... but mostly that. I am a member of the LGBTQ2+ communities. I'm writing a book about LGBTQ2+ inclusion because I want the world to be a better place for all members of the LGBTQ2+ communities, which also includes our allies.

As such, in addition to telling my own story, I share the stories of other LGBTQ2+ people, because a picture may be worth a thousand words, but a story... well, that's worth... something. I don't know what, but it doesn't matter. Stories help us move from theory into practice. They make it real.

I also recognize that in writing this book, there's a chance that I will infuriate some members of the LGBTQ2+ communities who will decry my work as the hubris of a cis white man who doesn't understand what it's like to be othered. And by "chance," I mean it's pretty much guaranteed. And they're right to some extent. I am those things (cis and white), but that doesn't change or diminish my experience. As much as I have experienced more than my fair share of discrimination because of my sexual orientation, I'm still a white cis man. My goal in adding my voice to this conversation is to create space for others. I'm not trying to suggest that (to quote Margaret Cho) I'm *the* gay, but I am *a* gay. I'm not the gay whisperer. But I have a perspective. Not only am I part of the LGBTQ2+ communities, but I have spent the better part of thirty years actively trying to make life better for my chosen LGBTQ2+ family.

I started my journey in this work when I was a wee lad and became the coordinator of the Lesbian and Gay Youth of Toronto (I know... the name is dated, but it was the '80s). I went on to work with a wide variety of LGBTQ2+ organizations, including the LGBT Youth Line, Canada's LGBT+ Chamber of Commerce (CGLCC), and many others. I became a "professional homosexual" in 2006 when I started working in diversity and inclusion, and in 2012, I founded the

Canadian Centre for Diversity and Inclusion (CCDI) and led that organization until 2021. I continue to work in the D&I space as a consultant. So, yeah—I've got cred.

My desire is, and has always been, to work toward a world where all people—regardless of and because of their sexuality, gender identity, gender expression, or frankly anything that makes them unique—can live their lives to their fullest potential. I want to ensure that people are not held back because of the things that make them the amazing people that they are. Hopefully *Alphabet Soup* will help you understand your role in doing just that.

1

MAKING IT ABOUT ME FOR A CHANGE

Openness may not completely **disarm prejudice**, but it's a good place to start.

JASON COLLINS, the first openly gay player in the National Basketball Association and in any major American team sport thought I would start out by sharing my journey toward becoming the dashing, handsome, sophisticated LGBTQ2+ man you see before you (at the back of the book, technically). I'm sure you've been wondering. Who wouldn't!

I was born in the early-to-mid-late 1900s, at a time when it was not only *not* appropriate to be openly gay; it was barely legal. We didn't have things like *Will and Grace* and Elton John. Well, we had Elton John, but he was still pretending he liked girls (insert laugh track here). At the time, homosexuals were reviled as evil and depraved. We were something to be feared and hated.

When I was nine years old, I attended Boyne River Natural Science School for a weeklong camp with my class from Maurice Cody Public School in Toronto, Ontario. It was a week of being in the outdoors and discovering nature. Not exactly my jam, but it wasn't optional, and I do recall wearing some supercute shorts. One day, I told my camp counselor that I liked boys, that I was gay.

I remember those words distinctly passing my lips, even now, some forty years later. I remember thinking that it was just who I was. It wasn't wrong. It wasn't something to be ashamed of. It was natural. I have no idea why I decided to share that little missive at that very moment, but I did. And oh, how I lived to regret it.

My counselor told my teacher, Mr. Hill. Mr. Hill told my principal, Mr. Reiner. Mr. Reiner told my parents, Mr. and Mrs. Bach (not how I commonly refer to them). And I got to spend an afternoon a week for a year at an institution now called the Hincks-Dellcrest Centre, talking to a psychiatrist about the horrible word I had uttered. Don't panic—I didn't undergo electroshock therapy or anything. Truthfully, we didn't talk about *that* word or me saying it, as I recall. We played the board game Sorry! and the therapist asked me questions about the boys I went to school with, who mercilessly bullied me. In the end, the therapist told my parents that I manifested no signs of homosexuality. He was wrong. Super-duper wrong. He clearly hadn't noticed my alter ego/imaginary friend, Madame Pink Unicorn, standing in the room with us. If nothing else, counseling helped me break my own behavior of apologizing for everything. #soCanadian

Keep in mind it was 1980. Homosexuality had only been removed as a psychological disorder from the *Diagnostic and Statistical Manual of Mental Disorders* (DSM) in 1973.[1] It was only five years prior to that, in 1967, when then Justice Minister Pierre Elliot Trudeau introduced Bill C-150 and uttered those famous words, "There's no place for the State in the bedrooms of the nation." In the United States, in 1961, Illinois effectively became the first state to decriminalize homosexuality by repealing its sodomy law. But if you're

American and thinking you took Canada to church, know that Texas's "homosexual conduct" law was not struck down by the US Supreme Court until 2003.

Other than the history lesson, the point is that it wasn't a terribly good time for LGBTQ2+ people anywhere. My parents' reaction was understandable, but they shouldn't have been surprised. I was not the butchest kid. I came out of the womb singing show tunes. In kindergarten, when all the boys were playing Construction, I was playing the role of "father" with all the girls in our adaptation of Family. It was a genius performance.

I was sensitive, kind, and gentle. I was an insatiable flirt (to hear my mother tell it, I would bat my eyes at women on the subway). All my friends were girls. I was not typically masculine. Not that my parents didn't try to butch me up. I believe we attempted every sport we could think of: soccer (the outfit was black and yellow... why they thought that combination would be appealing is beyond me); go-carts (I didn't like driving then, and I don't like driving now); softball (I have dreadful hand-eye coordination, and I'm not big on running); judo (pajamas in public?! 'Nuf said). So maybe not *every* sport, but a bunch—and none of them took. I did play volleyball in high school, but that was because I had a huge crush on the team captain. The point is that I wasn't destined to be "that kid"—the boy parents dream of. The boy who plays sports, gets good grades, loves his mother, respects his father, and grows up to marry his high school sweetheart and make lots of grandbabies.

But because of who I was, I faced endless bullying. I hated school because I knew that every day, I was going to face the mean kids. Mostly boys but a few girls too. They called me names. They beat me up. They made my life a living hell. And the teachers did nothing. Not that I blame them. Again, it was the '70s and '80s. They just didn't know better.

Ten years at Maurice Cody, two years at North Toronto Public School, and another two at Trinity College School (TCS), and the experience was the same. I was the queer punching bag. With every new school, I thought my reputation would not follow me, but it did. Not because there was some great conspiracy, but because I was who I was: Gay with a capital G.

I denied it as much as I could. I had girlfriends. I am not a gold-star gay: I had sex with women. I'm sort of a brushed-nickel gay. I spent a lot of time and energy trying to suppress something that was desperate to break free: me. I think of it now like Tony Award–winning Broadway great Patti LuPone trying to sing quietly in the chorus. Some things are just meant to be.

I was seventeen when I finally found the courage to utter the word "gay" again. In creative writing class in my senior year, we were working on a book of the school's history, and we had to interview alumni about their experiences. Stay with me ... there's a point.

I was assigned the Arts section (shocking, I know), and I had the opportunity to interview an alumnus named Jim. Jim had graduated the year before I arrived at the school, but I had heard rumors that he was a "homo." When the chance presented itself for me to interview him, I eagerly jumped at it. Let me paint a picture for you. He was coming to the school for the interview, and I decided we would meet in my room (TCS was an all-boys boarding school at the time, and my room was the *only* one on campus with a key—you couldn't dream this stuff up if you tried). I figured we would have more privacy in case the conversation "went there." I cleaned my room (more, since as a young gay boy I was impeccably clean) and used cologne samples from magazines to make it smell less like a seventeen-year-old boys' dungeon (my roommate felt that showering was just a suggestion). I dressed up—a navy blue brushed wool blazer, khaki chinos, and my favorite white Mexx turtleneck with a big, embroidered M in the center of the chest. I could have been the centerfold in a pictorial version of *Mein Kampf.*

I was terrified. We sat on my sofa and chatted for what felt like hours. At one point, when I was drunk on the conversation, I mustered up the courage to say, "May I ask you a personal question?"

Jim laughed. "Yes," he said.

"Are you gay?" I nearly whispered.

He laughed again and simply responded with another yes. I felt like I had been holding my breath for my whole life, and I could suddenly breathe again. "Oh, good," I said. "I think I may be too."

He hugged me for what seemed like an eternity. I remember that feeling like the most wonderful feeling I had ever experienced. He was the first person to tell me that who I was wasn't a bad thing. He was the first person to affirm my identity.

Sadly, that moment passed. Although Jim and I became great friends, decades of abuse had filled me with shame. I continued to date girls, claiming I was bisexual. In my twenties I amped up my drug use in an attempt to drown out my sorrow, leading to addiction that ended in detox and a lot of therapy.

Living in New York City, New York, in the '90s, I worked for a bank and was perpetually terrified of anyone discovering my little secret. New York State (and all US states at the time) had "at-will employment" (and some still have it), meaning you can be fired for pretty much any reason. The fact that I was a dancing queen would certainly be a reason to show me the door. So, I hid . . . as best I could.

Ironically, my private life juxtaposed my professional life. I was very active in the LGBTQ2+ communities. I volunteered for the New York City Gay and Lesbian Anti-Violence Project (now the New York City Anti-Violence Project, or AVP). I had large circles of LGBTQ2+ friends, went to dinner parties, and summered on Fire Island. But I spent a huge amount of energy making sure that what I did from sundown to sunup never saw the light of day.

It was a long time before I came out at work. Even when I was back in Canada, where I couldn't *legally* be discriminated against because of my sexual orientation, the damage had been done. I was perpetually afraid of people's reactions. It wasn't until 1999, when I was working for George

Smitherman, Ontario's first openly LGBTQ2+ Member of Provincial Parliament (MPP), that I decided to come out. Say what you will about George (so much to say... his nickname in the media was "Furious George"), but he held his head high and did not apologize to anyone for being who he was. I figured if he could do it, so could I.

I stopped lying. I stopped changing pronouns when I was speaking about my significant other. I stopped denying. I stopped hating myself. Don't get me wrong—the transformation wasn't instantaneous. I didn't wake up one morning suddenly a proud gay man, free of self-loathing. It took time. In fact, that work continues to this day. When you spend a significant part of your life being told that there's something wrong with you, you don't fix that overnight.

Now, as I crest fifty (I know—I don't look it. I have a surgeon on standby), I can say I'm proud of the person I've become. I am proud of the work I've done to make the world more inclusive for LGBTQ2+ people. I'm now recognized as a community "leader"—a term I use with great hesitance—putting myself out front in the fight for inclusion. In 2007, I started what has become Canada's leading LGBTQ2+ workplace inclusion organization (Pride at Work Canada) and elevated the conversation about sexuality and gender identity beyond pride festivals and cocktail parties. I've won awards for my work.

I'm not trying to brag. Believe it or not, I have a strong sense of humility. I share this as evidence of the contradiction between the young man who desperately tried to deny the truth and the man I've become, and of how the truth will set you free. In my case, it really did.

Sadly, my story isn't unique. It wasn't then, and it isn't now. Today we still see examples of homophobia, transphobia, and biphobia in day-to-day life. As of this writing, there are seventy-one countries where it is illegal to be gay or lesbian (they criminalize private consensual, same-sex sexual activity).[2] In eleven countries the penalty is death.[3] There are fifteen countries that have criminalized the gender identity and/or expression of Trans* and gender non-binary people.[4] The list includes Singapore, Saint Lucia, Morocco, and Barbados—countries I'm willing to bet you've heard of, possibly even visited.

And before you think these are just old laws that no one pays attention to, in April of 2019, the sultan of Brunei decided to *re*implement "stoning to death" as the punishment for consensual sex between two men.[5] The death penalty was already on the books, but no executions had taken place since 1957. I guess the sultan was feeling nostalgic for the good old days. Thankfully, a month later, because of a global outcry and pressure from people like George Clooney and Ellen DeGeneres, who called for a boycott of the sultan's luxury hotels, he reversed his position and said that the death penalty was off the table.[6] This guy is super generous! But keep in mind the law is still in place, so at any time he could change his mind and start the boulders rolling.

We in North America, and in most of the Western world, seem to think that life here is all rosy for LGBTQ2+ people;

looking down on the countries where it's still illegal to be LGBTQ2+ is all too easy. I mean, where are Bhutan and Eswatini anyway? Do they even have a Sandals Resort? Certainly not on my travel wish list.

But consider this: In the United States, the Federal Bureau of Investigation estimates that there are approximately seventy-five hundred hate crimes committed annually. And although we love the FBI (#goFBI), the National Crime Victimization Survey (NCVS, administered by the US Census Bureau, based on self-reporting) suggests that Americans experience closer to two hundred thousand hate crimes every year.[7] Now consider that research shows that 20 percent of hate crimes are motivated by anti-LGBTQ2+ bias.[8] Approximately 49 percent of LGBTQ2+ Americans live in states that don't have hate crime laws covering sexual orientation and gender identity.[9]

Canada's a little better by the numbers. According to Statistics Canada, there were 1,798 hate crimes reported in 2018, of which 173 (or just under 10 percent) were motivated by sexual orientation. The key word here is *reported*. Canada doesn't have anything similar to the NCVS. I could go on and on with the evidence. The point: while it sucks to be LGBTQ2+ in Jamaica and Indonesia, it ain't all peaches and cream for LGBTQ2+ folks in North America either.

So, now you know. And knowing is half the battle. My passion for LGBTQ2+ inclusion is deeply personal because I want to leave a world where little kids don't have to hide or be ashamed of who they are. I wrote this book with the simple objective of engaging people—specifically cis straight people—in creating a more inclusive world for LGBTQ2+ people. I've included very practical recommendations that individuals and organizations can implement to ensure that your workplaces are more productive, your schools are more inclusive, and your communities are more resilient.

Key Takeaways

- In seventy-one countries in the world, being gay or lesbian is illegal. In fifteen countries, being Trans* or gender diverse is illegal.

- Thousands of LGBTQ2+ people experience hate crimes in North America every year, totaling between 10 and 20 percent of all hate crimes.

- Although North America's LGBTQ2+ inclusion has come a long way, people still experience homophobia, transphobia, and biphobia.

2

BREAKING DOWN THE ALPHABET

If I wait for someone else
to validate my existence,
it will mean that I'm
shortchanging myself.

ZANELE MUHOLI, an LGBTQ2+
South African activist and artist

To start this journey of learning, you need to understand what a bunch of words mean. Books have words, and if you don't understand the words, you won't understand the book, as I learned when I attempted to read *The Art of War* by Sun Tzu in its original Chinese. I, apparently, don't understand Chinese, so I was a little lost.

Below I provide a glossary of sorts, and I'd encourage you to take a gander. The language is constantly evolving—by the time the ink is dry on this book, it will have changed. So even if you are up on LGBTQ2+ issues, in reading this chapter, you may learn a few things. If you're new to the topic, this chapter will at least help you figure out what your kids mean when they tell you they don't identify with labels.

I have adapted much of these definitions from Sam Killermann's "Comprehensive* List of LGBTQ+ Vocabulary Definitions."[1] I was confused by the name of Sam's site, It's Pronounced Metrosexual, because, of course, I always assumed he was a supercute proud member of the LGBTQ2+ communities... until I watched his TED Talk entitled "Understanding the Complexities of Gender," in which the first words out of his mouth are, "I'm not gay."[2] Turns out,

Sam is a metrosexual (meaning he's straight and cis but has style). #crushed

Regardless of this tragic revelation, Sam has produced some amazing resources on this topic, and I have leveraged them to create this glossary for you. Thanks, Sam. And if you ever decide to explore your sexuality... call me.

Be forewarned. Your brain is about to hurt. I'm about to throw a lot of definitions at you. I've organized them around topics, and I've tried to keep them light and fun. But these words are going to crawl into the nether regions of your brain and install themselves there, which will ultimately mean you will use some cognitive energy as you familiarize yourself with them. Isn't learning awesome? Just keep in mind that these terms and definitions are constantly changing, so keep yourself up to date by visiting Sam's site regularly.

The Many Versions of the Alphabet

I would be remiss if I didn't start by explaining the initial-ism (like an acronym but the difference is you can't make a word out of it—PETA and NASA are acronyms; CIA and LGBTQ2+ are initialisms—look at you learning!). LGBTQ2+ stands for Lesbian, Gay, Bisexual, Trans-identified, Queer, Two-spirit, plus.

This is one version of an initialism that has many variants, including but not limited to:

- LGB (Lesbian, Gay, Bisexual)

- LGBT (Lesbian, Gay, Bisexual, Trans-identified)

- LGBTQ (Lesbian, Gay, Bisexual, Trans-identified, Queer)

- LGBT+ (Lesbian, Gay, Bisexual, Trans-identified, plus)

- LGBT* (Lesbian, Gay, Bisexual, Trans-identified, asterisk)

- LGBTQIA (Lesbian, Gay, Bisexual, Trans-identified, Queer, Intersex, Allies)

- LGBTTQQIAAP (Lesbian, Gay, Bisexual, Transgender, Transsexual, Queer, Questioning, Intersex, Ally, Asexual, Pansexual)

- LGBTTIQQ2SA (Lesbian, Gay, Bisexual, Transgender, Transsexual, Intersex, Queer, Questioning, Two-spirit, Allies)

- LGBTQIAGNC (Lesbian, Gay, Bisexual, Transgender, Queer, Intersex, Asexual, Gender Non-conforming)

- LGBTIP2SQQAPKA (Lesbian, Gay, Bisexual, Transgender, Intersex, Pansexual, Two-spirit, Queer, Questioning, Asexual, Polyamorous, Kinky, Allies)

- LGBTIQCAPGNGFNBA (Lesbian, Gay, Bisexual, Transgender, Intersex, Questioning, Curious, Asexual, Pansexual, Gender Non-conforming, Gender-fluid, Non-binary, Androgynous)

No, I did not make any of those up. And yes, there are more. Lots more. Far too many to print in one book. This book isn't *À la recherche du temps perdu* (rando factoid: the longest book ever written, with 9.6 million characters), so I've just listed the more "common" initialisms I could find. Over the years, the initialism has grown and adapted in an attempt to welcome all into the tent so they can find their identity and feel like they belong.

Although I laud and support this effort, it may be verging on the absurd. Try saying LGBTIQCAPGNGFNBA three times fast. It's not something you can say in casual conversation. By the time you get through it, your audience will have moved on to the endless shrimp buffet. Using a shorter initialism like LGBT, LGBTQ, LGBTQI, or LGBTQ2+ is perfectly acceptable, as long as you understand that when you use that initialism, you're talking about a complex set of identities that go well beyond those few letters.

I use LGBTQ2+ because the Canadian government uses LGBTQ2 to be inclusive of people who identify as queer and our Indigenous cousins. I added the plus sign to ensure that everyone knows they have a place in my big rainbow-colored tent.

Sexuality

Now let's look at words that relate to sexuality. Here I include the more commonly known words. This is by no means a definitive list, but it's a good sampling of the menu. I also want to point out that this isn't a dictionary, and I'm not the gay buddha. There may be other definitions for these words, but this is a good starting point on the roller coaster of your LGBTQ2+ *edumacation.*

Sexual Orientation

Throughout this book, when I refer to "sexual orientation," I mean the type of sexual, romantic, and/or emotional attraction one feels for others, generally but not always defined based on the gender of the person and of the people a person is attracted to. Sometimes people use the term "sexual preference," but I strongly discourage its use. It suggests a person has a choice in who they're sexually attracted to, and I assure you, you don't. Denial doesn't make attraction go away.

Romantic or Emotional Attraction versus Sexual Attraction

Romantic or emotional attraction refers to a person's desire to engage in romantically or emotionally intimate behavior (for example, dating, relationships, marriage). Sexual attraction describes a person's desire to engage in sexual activity. It's important to note that the two are not always the same. It is possible for a person to be romantically attracted to someone but have no sexual attraction to that person, and vice versa.

Homosexual

The term "homosexual" describes a person who is solely (or primarily) emotionally, physically, and/or sexually attracted to members of the same sex or gender. It is a medical term and is now widely considered stigmatizing because of its history as a category of mental illness, and it is not commonly used. And it's just awkward to say in casual conversation: "Oh yes, I have the most wonderful homosexual friends." #notcute

Heterosexual/Straight

A person who is attracted solely (or primarily) to members of the opposite sex or gender. Now, why is heterosexual included here? Because guess what... it's a sexual orientation. We sometimes forget that.

Lesbian

It is generally agreed that the L in the initialism stands for "lesbian," which is a person who identifies as a woman who is solely (or primarily) attracted romantically, emotionally, and/or sexually to others who identify as women.

Gay

The term "gay" is *commonly* used to describe a person who identifies as a man who is solely (or primarily) attracted romantically, emotionally, and/or sexually to other men. That said, it is also sometimes used by women and people of other genders. At times, it is also used as a catchall when describing the LGBTQ2+ communities—for example, when saying things like "gay pride." This isn't a good thing. Gays don't have their own pride celebration. It's LGBTQ2+ pride.

Bisexual

"Bisexual" is the term used to describe a person who experiences romantic, emotional, and/or sexual attraction to both men and women. Bisexuality does not mean a person's attraction is equally split. Sometimes this term is used interchangeably with "pansexual," but some would argue that bisexuality tends to be more specific to cisgender people.

Pansexual

The term "pansexual" is relatively new to the lexicon (sometimes appearing in the initialism as "P") and is used to describe a person who experiences romantic, emotional, and/or sexual feelings toward members of all gender identities and expressions. Sometimes the term is shortened simply to "pan."

Asexual

"Asexual," sometimes represented by an "A" in the initialism, describes a person that experiences little or no sexual attraction to others and/or lacks interest in sexual relationships or behavior. Asexuality exists on a continuum and includes people who experience no sexual attraction and those who experience low levels or sexual attraction only under specific conditions. You may also hear the term "demisexual," which tends to be considered part of asexuality. Demisexual people tend to be sexually attracted only to someone they have an emotional bond with.

Aromantic

A person who identifies as "aromantic" may experience little or no romantic attraction to others and/or lack interest in romantic relationships or behavior. Like asexuality, aromanticism exists on a continuum, from people who experience no romantic attraction to those who experience low levels of romantic attraction, or romantic attraction only under certain conditions. Sometimes you will hear the term "demiromantic," which tends to be considered part of aromanticism. Similar to demisexual people, demiromantic people tend to develop romantic feelings for a person only once they have a strong emotional connection to them.

Polyamorous

The word "polyamorous" refers to the practice of having ethical, honest, and consensual non-monogamous relationships (in other words, relationships that may include multiple partners). There is a lot of contention about the concept of polyamory within the LGBTQ2+ communities, let alone how straight cis people feel about it. But it is a reality, and it's becoming more common to hear about it in conversation. In essence, it's the ability to love and be in a relationship with more than one person at the same time.

MSM/WSW

MSM and WSW are abbreviations for "men who have sex with men" and "women who have sex with women." These distinguish sexual behavior from sexual identity and can apply regardless of what sexual orientation a person identifies with. For instance, a man may identify as straight, but that doesn't mean he's not interested in having sex with men. We often see MSM used in the HIV/AIDS space when talking about blood donation. At the time of writing, in Canada and the United States, the rules around blood donation for MSMs are changing.

Heteronormativity

The terms "heteronormative" and "heteronormativity" are meant to define the assumption that everyone is heterosexual until proved otherwise, and that heterosexuality is superior to all other sexualities. Heteronormativity can lead to feelings of invisibility and stigmatizing of other sexualities. For example, when you learn that a woman is married, if you ask her what her *husband's* name is as opposed to what her *spouse's* name is, that's heteronormative, as is assuming that only masculine men and feminine women are straight.

Heterosexism

"Heterosexism" is a behavior that grants preferential treatment to straight people and reinforces the idea that heterosexuality is somehow better. The debate around marriage equality, which is still occurring in many countries that have already legalized same-sex marriage, is heterosexist in its nature. It assumes that the act of marriage should be reserved for straight cis people. I disagree. I feel like LGBTQ2+ have the right to be unhappy too.

Gender

Now let's take a look at words that relate specifically to "gender." Again, this is not a "complete" list, largely because I don't know that there *could be* a complete list. For some readers, this is going to be new territory, and the conversation is quite complex. There is a *lot* of confusion about the differences between each identity, largely because, in the initialism, we tend to group a significant number of gender identities and expressions under one letter: T. Don't be afraid if you're new to this. Take it slow. I'll be gentle.

Gender Identity

Let's start with the fundamental concept of "gender identity." A person's gender identity is the *internal* perception of their gender, and how they identify, based on how much they align or don't align with what they understand their options for gender to be. Often this is confused with anatomical sex or sex assigned at birth, which it is not.

Gender Expression

"Gender expression" is related to gender identity but can be quite different. A person's gender expression is the *external* presentation of their gender, through a combination of their clothing, grooming, demeanor, social behavior, and other factors, generally described on scales of masculinity and femininity. A person may identify as a gender that *does not* align with their sex assigned at birth but may present in a manner that *does* align with that sex.

Gender Non-Conforming

The term "gender non-conforming" is used to indicate a nontraditional gender identity or expression of a person who identifies as being outside the gender binary of man and woman. A masculine cisgender woman may identify as being gender non-conforming, as may a non-binary person whose gender expression is stereotypically feminine.

Cisgender

"Cisgender" describes a person whose sex assigned at birth and gender identity match up. Meaning, if you look at your naked body in the mirror and think that all the parts are where they're supposed to be, you are likely cisgender. The term "cisgender" is derived from Latin, and it means "on this side of." Cisgender can also be shortened to "cis."

Trans*

"Trans*," or "Trans-identified," is an umbrella term meant to include several identities that fall outside of socially defined gender norms. Similar to "cis," the word "Trans*" is derived from Latin and means "on the other side of." Sometimes you will see Trans* with an asterisk (as you will throughout this book) to indicate that you're speaking about the larger group of Trans* people, including non-binary identities.

Transgender

"Transgender" is a term that has a mixed use. Sometimes it's used to describe a person who does not identify with their sex assigned at birth. Other times, it's used to describe a person who is in the process of transitioning, or has transitioned, their gender through some form of gender affirmation surgery. Unlike the term "transsexual," "transgender" has become an umbrella term used to describe people who do not identify with the binary of male and female.

Transsexual

Historically, "transsexual" was a medical term used to indicate a difference between one's gender identity and sex assigned at birth. More specifically, the term generally identifies a person who undergoes some form of medical changes, such as hormone replacement or gender affirmation surgery, to alter their anatomy to align more closely with their gender identity. Unlike "transgender," "transsexual" refers to a specific group and is not an umbrella term.

Transvestite

A "transvestite" (sometimes called a "cross-dresser") is a person who dresses as the opposite sex than the one they were assigned at birth for many different reasons, including relaxation, fun, and sexual gratification. It doesn't mean they identify as that sex or that they will pursue any form of transition.

Gender Non-binary

"Gender non-binary," or simply "non-binary," is a term used by people whose gender is outside the binary of man and woman. It is a spectrum of identities that fall under the Trans* umbrella. Non-binary people may identify as having two or more genders, having no gender, being a third or other gender, or fluctuating between genders. Some people also consider the term "genderqueer" to be synonymous. Non-binary people may prefer to use different pronouns, which I will discuss later in the book.

Agender, Gender-Neutral, or Genderless

Someone who identifies as "agender" has no (or very little) connection to the traditional norms around gender. The terms "agender," "gender-neutral," or "genderless" are some-times confused or used interchangeably with "androgyny," which describes a person that has both masculine and femi-nine characteristics.

Bi-gender

A "bi-gender" person is one who swings between "woman" and "man" gender-based behavior and identities, identifying with two genders.

FtM/F2M and MtF/M2F

These are abbreviations for female-to-male or male-to-female and relate specifically to a person's gender transition. These terms are largely unused in society outside of medical treatment where, again, gender is sometimes considered a binary.

Transman or Transwoman

"Transman" and "transwoman" are used to describe a man or a woman who has transitioned genders—socially, medically, and/or legally—to the gender they identify with, which is indicated by the second part of the term (in other words, "-man" or "-woman"). Not all people who are Trans* identify with this term and may simply identify as a man or a woman.

Transitioning

"Transitioning" refers to the process of people changing aspects of themselves (such as their appearance, name, pronouns, body) to be more in line with the gender they know themselves to be. Some other terms you may have heard are "sex reassignment surgery" or "gender reassignment surgery," but a more welcoming and inclusive alternative term is "gender affirmation surgery." Keep in mind that not all Trans* people choose to have any form of surgery to alter their bodies.

Genderqueer

"Genderqueer" is a term sometimes used by people who do not identify with the binary of man and woman, and it is sometimes used as an umbrella term for many gender non-conforming or non-binary identities.

Gender Fabulous

You've probably never heard this one before, and I can't claim responsibility for it. Two friends—Kai Scott and Drew Dennis, who are fantastic consultants in the gender space—came up with it. The first time I heard it, I just thought it was such a great way to describe people. #twosnaps

Misgendering

"Misgendering" a person is the process of incorrectly assuming knowledge of a person's gender or gender identity, based on visible characteristics and assumptions, as opposed to asking a person how they identify, such as asking their pronouns.

Cisnormativity

"Cisnormativity" is similar to heteronormativity in that it is the assumption that everyone is cisgender and that cisgender identities are superior to Trans* identities and people.

Cissexism

Similar to heterosexism, "cissexism" is preferential treatment of cisgender people, reinforcing the idea that being cisgender is somehow "normal." Like when President Trump decided to reintroduce the ban on Trans* people serving in the military. Because that seemed logical and worthy of his time. (Insert eye roll here.)

A Little Bit of Both

Just to really confuse you, there are some terms that can be used when speaking about sexual orientation *or* gender identity or expression ... or both! Just because your head doesn't hurt enough at this point.

Fluid

The term "fluid" is usually used to describe a person who feels their gender is fluid, or their sexuality is fluid and does not fit under any other label.

Queer

"Queer" is an umbrella term to describe individuals who don't identify as straight and/or cisgender. Historically, "queer" was used as a pejorative, but in recent years it has been reclaimed, particularly among younger people, as a form of empowerment. Some people who identify as part of the LGBTQ2+ communities loathe the term, and some people love it. But just like the size of my ass, not liking it doesn't make it go away.

Questioning

The term "questioning" describes a person who is unsure about, or is exploring, their sexual orientation or gender.

Two-Spirit

"Two-spirit" is traditionally used by Native American and Indigenous people to identify individuals who possess qualities or fulfill roles of both feminine and masculine genders. In some cases, a Two-spirit person may be referring to their sexual orientation, or their gender identity, or both. It is included in the initialism as "2" or "2s."

Closeted

The term "closeted" is used to describe an individual who is not open to themselves or others about their sexuality or gender. A person may be "in the closet" for a multitude of reasons, including fear or safety. Like when Matt Damon played Owen in the *Will and Grace* episode "A Chorus Lie."[3] Owen was straight, but he really loved choral singing, so he pretended to be gay so he could audition for the Manhattan Gay Men's Chorus. Admittedly that was a long explanation for what should be a simple term, but I love that episode, so there you go. You're welcome.

Coming Out

"Coming out" (sometimes referred to as "coming out of the closet") is the process of accepting and/or sharing one's sexuality or gender with others. Like when Matt Damon's character Owen had to come out as straight. Which we're all still sad about.

Passing Privilege

The concept of "passing privilege" is about how an LGBTQ2+ person might pass as straight and/or as cis if they don't declare that they are not so. A Trans* person might pass as the gender they identify with. A lesbian might pass as straight. Like Matt Damon. Who is not a lesbian, to be clear.

SOGI

The acronym "SOGI" is short for Sexual Orientation and Gender Identity. You will sometimes see it in place of LGBTQ2+ because it's meant to be inclusive of all sexualities and genders, including straight cisgender people.

Biology

Differentiating terminology related to a person's biology is important. Although there are only two terms under this heading, I include them because people often misunderstand that they speak to biology and *not* identity.

Anatomical, or Biological, Sex

"Anatomical sex" is a medical term that refers to the biological characteristics used to classify a person as female, male, or intersex. You may hear other versions of this term, including "sex," "biological sex," or "sex assigned at birth."

Intersex

"Intersex" is a medical term used to describe a person born with some combination of chromosomes, gonads, hormones, internal sex organs, and genitals of both male and female. Formerly you may have heard the term "hermaphrodite," but it is quite outdated and derogatory.

There are several variants of how intersex can present, but according to the Intersex Society of North America, approximately one in one hundred births have some form of intersex characteristics—meaning their bodies differ from the standard male and female.

One correction, for the record: In my first book, *Birds of All Feathers* (which I know you've read), I said that intersex births run between one in 1,500 and one in 2,000. To be clear, I'm not contradicting myself; I've just got more data now. The one in one hundred births refers to all potential sex variants, such as not-XX and not-XY (one in 1,666 births); Klinefelter's syndrome, or XXY (one in 1,000 births); or ovotestis (one in 83,000 births).[4] Look at us learning together!

For Your Consideration

There are a few more words that don't relate specifically to sexuality or gender but are an important part of the conversation.

Ally

An "ally" is a straight and/or cisgender person who supports and respects members of the LGBTQ2+ communities. Sometimes you may also hear the term "advocate." The difference between being an ally and an advocate, in my humble opinion, is that advocates tend to play a more active role in LGBTQ2+ inclusion. I differentiate by saying "armchair ally" versus "active ally." You're going to hear more about allies later on in the book.

Biphobia

"Biphobia" describes negative feelings and/or beliefs that a person may have or express toward bisexual people.

Homophobia

Similar to "biphobia," "homophobia" describes negative feelings and/or beliefs that a person may have or express toward gay and lesbian people. It is also sometimes used as an umbrella term related to negative feelings and/or beliefs toward all LGBTQ2+ people, although using more specific terms to describe specific types of phobias (for example, biphobia and transphobia) is preferable.

Transphobia

"Transphobia" describes negative feelings and/or beliefs that a person may have or express toward Trans* and gender non-binary people. It is an umbrella term to describe such behavior toward people of all different genders.

Who Cares?

Now that your head is full of words that you may or may not have heard before, I would be remiss if I didn't talk about why any of these words matter.

Straight cisgender people's experiences of the world don't resemble the experiences of LGBTQ2+ people in any way. Look around, and the world tells you that the default is straight and cisgender. Advertising, television, movies, politicians—everywhere you turn, straight cisgender people are sent this sometimes subliminal, sometimes overt message that they are "normal." If you are straight and cisgender, you don't have to question. You just are.

For people who identify as being part of the LGBTQ2+ communities, it's nowhere near that simple. The journey to their identity is filled with a great deal of self-exploration and introspection. When they look around, they often struggle to see themselves modeled in the world. When they do figure it out, they want the world to recognize them as *themselves*, and they certainly don't want to have to fight as people try to push them back into the closet from whence they came.

Terminology matters because it's personal. It's part of who an LGBTQ2+ person is. It can take a long time to come to terms with the terminology, and when people don't refer to your identity properly (like calling a Trans* person a cross-dresser)—or worse, when people refuse to refer to you by your identity (like referring to a Trans* person by their sex assigned at birth and not by their gender identity)—it can have an unintended (or potentially intended) negative impact. It can leave a person feeling invisible, or it can further embed a person's feelings of self-loathing.

Some people struggle to use a person's pronouns, and I'll admit it can be difficult. When a former colleague's daughter came out as non-binary, we all struggled to switch pronouns when referring to them. Many times, we caught ourselves saying "she" or "her" instead of "they" or "them." Thankfully, never to their face. Changing terminology is hard. It requires us to not rely on the scripts of our unconscious brain. It requires us to think.

Some people simply refuse to respect people's identity. Jordan Peterson from the University of Toronto flatly refused to use the pronouns of his students, saying, "If the standard transsexual person wants to be regarded as he or she, my sense is I'll address you according to the part that you appear to be playing."[5] Aside from my general distaste for Dr. Peterson's *craptastic* attitude, he's not alone. I can't imagine he wants to change, or that he cares whom he hurts along the way... as long as *he* isn't inconvenienced.

But we change all the time. Let's consider names. Champion boxer Muhammad Ali was born Cassius Marcellus Clay Jr. but changed his name when he converted to Islam. Do you think anyone would insist on referring to him as Cassius just because that's what they had always called him? Not if they wanted to keep their teeth.

My name is Michael. I have always been Michael. I am never Mike. I don't act like a Mike. I don't sound like a Mike. I don't identify as a Mike. When people attempt to shorten my name, instead of referring to me by the name I have introduced myself with, I correct them, and no one gets offended.

The important thing to remember about terminology is that *it's not about you*. It's not about what you like. It's not about how you think of a person. It's about how the other person identifies, and it's about showing them respect by acknowledging their identity and referring to them by the verbiage that they feel reflects them the most.

Key Takeaways

- Sex and gender are not the same thing. Nor are sexuality and gender identity.

- There are a multitude of identities that a person can identify with.

- The important thing is to respect the individual and understand that identity is about how they identify, not how you identify them.

3

UNDERSTANDING SEXUALITY, IDENTITY, AND EXPRESSION

I mean, if **Native languages have no gender**, then why should we?

TOMSON HIGHWAY, Indigenous Canadian playwright, novelist, and children's author

O key dokey. Now that you've got all those words taking up space in your head, let's further explore a few of them more deeply. As I have mentioned, sexual orientation and gender identity are not the same thing. Understanding this is a critical prerequisite for creating safe space—and this is usually where straight cisgender people start staring blankly and drooling, or they curl up in the fetal position. So, let's see if we can't unclench you.

If you are straight and cisgender, you've likely never had to question your identity (well, maybe that one time in college). Boys are boys. Girls are girls. Boys like girls and girls like boys. It's pretty simple. But imagine if a doctor said you were a girl, and no fiber of your being felt like a girl, and you were attracted to girls? And there goes the head explosion again.

If you don't understand the difference between attraction, identity, and expression, you risk misgendering someone or making assumptions about their relationship and the like, which signals that you haven't done the work and LGBTQ2+ people are not in a safe, inclusive environment.

I've said it before, but it bears repeating: Sam Killermann's "Comprehensive* List of LGBTQ+ Vocabulary Definitions," available on his wonderful website, It's Pronounced Metro-sexual, is bar none the best at breaking down the differences between sexual attraction, identity, and expression.[1] He uses a simple and incredibly effective tool to explain it all: the Genderbread Person (GP). The first time I saw the Genderbread Person, I felt I should've had a V8. It's such a creative way of illustrating this complex topic. So, let's break it down.

It's All a Spectrum

The first and most important thing to note is that everything we're talking about—sexuality, identity, expression, and so on—is on a spectrum. There is no right/wrong, black/white, yin/yang, peanut butter/chocolate to the conversations around attraction, identity, and expression. They can be one thing or another, somewhere in between, or not at all. Sexual orientation and gender are not binary. Even sex assigned at birth is a spectrum from female to male, with intersex somewhere in between. An intersex person can be born with more female physiology or more male physiology. No one is the same. We're all snowflakes.

As is indicated on the Genderbread Person figure, the identities under the categories of gender identity, gender expression, and anatomical sex run from a ⊘ symbol (meaning a lack of something) to an identity on the right. Likewise, sexual and romantic attraction can go from ⊘ to attraction to someone who identifies or presents as a woman or a man; feminine or masculine; female or male. The ⊘ symbol helps

THE GENDERBREAD PERSON

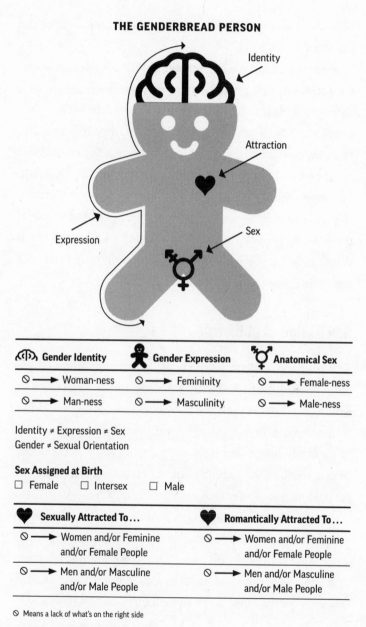

Identity

Attraction

Expression

Sex

Gender Identity	Gender Expression	Anatomical Sex
⊘ ⟶ Woman-ness	⊘ ⟶ Femininity	⊘ ⟶ Female-ness
⊘ ⟶ Man-ness	⊘ ⟶ Masculinity	⊘ ⟶ Male-ness

Identity ≠ Expression ≠ Sex
Gender ≠ Sexual Orientation

Sex Assigned at Birth
☐ Female ☐ Intersex ☐ Male

♥ Sexually Attracted To...	♥ Romantically Attracted To...
⊘ ⟶ Women and/or Feminine and/or Female People	⊘ ⟶ Women and/or Feminine and/or Female People
⊘ ⟶ Men and/or Masculine and/or Male People	⊘ ⟶ Men and/or Masculine and/or Male People

⊘ Means a lack of what's on the right side

CONCEPT BY SAM KILLERMANN, GENDERBREAD.ORG

us understand that *not* identifying with either side of the spectrum is possible.

Keep this in mind when engaging with others. Our brains tend to categorize people into groupings based on what we can see, leveraging outdated and inaccurate stereotypes about identity. If you see a man who isn't hyper-masculine, you may assume he's gay. That's not necessarily true. If you see a person who you think looks like a woman, you could be misgendering them based on the way they look. Perhaps that person identifies as non-binary and uses the pronoun they/them, but you may not know that by looking at them. Whether or not someone fits a stereotype has little to do with their being one thing or another.

Sex Assigned at Birth

Sex assigned at birth happens at the very beginning—like, when you're born. At birth, a doctor, nurse, doula, a taxi driver (or whoever pulls the baby out) looks down and determines: male or female. Usually you hear that person exclaim, "It's a boy!" but in fact what they should say is, "It's male," because what they're really talking about is anatomical sex (male) and not gender (boy).

This is the act of assigning sex to the child. It is based on a visual assessment. I see vagina, I yell, "Girl!"; I see penis, I yell, "Boy!" (I really do—every time I see a penis. It's quite annoying.) There are times when a child is born with an obvious sex variation, and that's when they bring in a specialist in sex differentiation to sort it out. Truthfully, the visual assignment isn't entirely accurate because you need to look under the hood to be certain. Babies have hoods, right?

The point is, there are a lot of kids out there who may actually be intersex but go through life thinking they are one sex or another, which may not be accurate.

Anatomical Sex Is Not Identity

Anatomical sex (not to be confused with the act of sex ... and let's face it, who isn't acting when they have sex) refers to the physical characteristics that we are born with, or what develops as we age. Genitals, breasts, body hair, body shape, voice, and so on. These characteristics are biological and beyond our personal control. You can't will your penis to be larger (not that I would ever have to worry about that ☺). It is what it is.

You can alter your anatomical sex through surgery and medication, which is what some (not all) Trans* and gender fabulous people do to ensure their outsides match their insides. But this would not happen on its own.

Gender Identity Is How You Identify

Gender identity is just how it sounds—it's how you identify. It's how you see yourself when you look in the mirror. You may look in the mirror and see the gender you identify with, and then again, you may not. A good friend once explained it to me by saying that when she stood naked in front of the mirror, she couldn't comprehend why there was a penis between her legs. It wasn't supposed to be there. Her brain and her body weren't aligned.

Some would argue that gender identity is not about "identification" at all but is about who a person is. One doesn't *identify* as a woman as much as one *is* a woman. I get that and feel like we may be in furious agreement. The important message here, particularly for people who are cisgender, is that gender identity is not who you *want* to be but who you *are*.

Gender Expression Is How You Present

Gender expression is equally self-explanatory in that it's how you express or present yourself to the world. That may be through your appearance, mannerisms, or other actions. If you identify as a man, regardless of your sex assigned at birth, you may have facial hair, wear suits, keep your hair short, and have a lower timbre to your voice. If you identify as a woman, you may have longer hair, wear makeup, shave your legs, and wear high heels. To be clear, these are gender stereotypes. Not all women shave their legs or wear high heels, obviously, but I'm using those stereotypes to make a point.

Sometimes your gender expression matches your gender identity. Sometimes it doesn't. This is usually where cisgender people have the most trouble: when a person's expression doesn't align with societal expectations of what masculine or feminine should look like.

When I was a child growing up, my father ran a company and employed two women on his team—Jean and Rose. Jean and Rose were lesbians, and in fact, they identified as bull dykes... or at least that's the label that society had applied to them. They were not stereotypically feminine in any way. They allowed their body hair to grow where it grew. Rose (when I first met her) had a cropped, almost military-like haircut. Jean rode a motorcycle. Neither one would know what to do with lipstick if it poked them in the eye.

I shan't explain the origins of the term "bull dyke" (because it's a bit offensive, and that's what Wikipedia is for) but suffice it to say that it dates back to the early 1900s and referred to lesbians who were "rough" and exhibited more traditionally masculine traits. Society couldn't see them as women, so they used a derogatory name for them, which ultimately some women have chosen to embrace and reclaim. Like Jean and Rose. Who are also fabulous!

Sexual Attraction Is About Who You Desire

Sexual attraction can be different from romantic attraction in that it's about who you're sexually attracted to. As you can see from the GB figure (page 51), you can be attracted to women and/or feminine people and/or female people. So, you may be attracted to a feminine person or someone who identifies as female but whose anatomical sex is different. The same is the case for men and/or masculine people and/or male people. You also may not experience sexual attraction, or you might only experience it under certain circumstances.

I've known men who were quite masculine and identified as gay, but they were sexually attracted to more feminine men. I've also known masculine gay men who were repulsed by anything that was slightly feminine in a man. Regardless of the reasons why, they are attracted to whom they're attracted to (and I'm not going to get into the psychology of this, or discuss internalized homophobia, because this book can't get any longer).

Romantic Attraction Is Not Necessarily Sexual

Unlike sexual attraction, romantic attraction is about who you're romantically or emotionally attracted to. It is possible to be romantically or emotionally attracted to a person but not sexually attracted to them.

Many years ago, I knew a married couple. I forget their names, but let's call them Aphrodite and Zeus—a cisgender woman and a cisgender man. When I met them, my gaydar went off like a five-alarm fire (yes, gaydar is really a thing). I thought, there is no way these two people are married. He's gay and she's a lesbian.

And I was right and wrong at the same time. He was gay. She was a lesbian. And they were married. They were romantically in love, but for them romance didn't involve sex, and so they didn't have sex. Some might look at their relationship and think of them as really good friends, but it went beyond that. They had an arrangement: she was allowed to have sex with women, and he was allowed to have sex with men. But that's where the dalliances ended. It may not have made sense to some, but it worked for them. Imagine having the love, support, and respect of a spouse and not having to do the horizontal mambo-jambo with them. Talk about the perfect marriage.

Let Go of the Binary

All this is to say that this is a very complex, layered topic. It is not simple. It is not binary. People are made up of a lot of different, and sometimes seemingly contradictory, parts. If your goal is to create an inclusive space for LGBTQ2+ folks, you need to ensure that you are letting go of the old concept that there is only Adam and Eve. I'm not saying that's easy. Far from it. Our society has been built on the stereotypes of masculine and feminine.

Consider this: In every province and territory in Canada, and in every state in the United States, when you start a job, you are required to complete tax forms that include your sex, and you still only have the binary options of male and female, in most (if not all) jurisdictions. Why does that even matter? Why does the government need to know your sex? What are they doing with that information?

Truthfully, they don't need to know. Collecting this data is, at best, dated in its approach. Once upon a time, back before the invention of the car and the talkies, sex was an indicator of certain things—like life expectancy—but that was because many women didn't have jobs outside the home.

Now, we could have a great debate about life expectancy and sex, and the mitigating factors, but the point is, a few things have changed since then. And the systems we are working within are still binary. We see it every day. Recently I booked a flight. I was asked my "gender" and given the options of "male" and "female." Frankly, considering the company with which I booked said flight, I expected better, because they are very advanced on the subject, but said company is also asking the questions based on the legislation, which is controlled by government. It's super complex and intricate. The challenge we face is how to blow up the infrastructure and rebuild it in a way that is inclusive of all people.

Key Takeaways

- There are vast differences between attraction, identity, and expression.

- Each identity is a spectrum.

- Understanding the complexity of the conversation about attraction, identity, and expression is a prerequisite for creating LGBTQ2+ inclusive spaces.

4

STRAIGHT AND CIS UNTIL PROVED OTHERWISE

I've never been interested in **being invisible** and erased.

LAVERNE COX, African American actor, producer, and activist, as well as the first openly Trans* actor to be featured on the cover of *Time* magazine, to be nominated for a Primetime Emmy Award, and to win a Daytime Emmy Award

Here's a fun fact: you are straight and cisgender until proved otherwise. That is not my opinion. It is a fact. Straight cisgender people never have to decide if they should come out. But every LGBTQ2+ person carries the burden of coming out to every person they ever meet, or at the very least they have to *decide* if they want to come out. The words "heteronormativity" and "cisnormativity" refer to that kind of dynamic. There's a default, and it is *not* gender fabulous!

Case in point: back in 2010, just after I got married, I called my bank because I wanted to add my husband to my contact information. That's what you do when you get married: you start to comingle things so that you have something fun to do when your marriage falls apart... un-mingle them. But I digress.

I explained to the bright, chipper woman (I am assuming she was a woman based on her voice and her name, Barbara) that I had just gotten married and wanted to add my spouse to my contact information. Barbara immediately responded with, "Congratulations. What's your wife's name?"

I paused and let out a little sigh. "His name is Mike," I replied.

Barbara was immediately flustered and apologized profusely. I honestly forget sometimes that, because I'm a not-so-typically-masculine man, people don't just assume I'm gay based on stereotypes. Truthfully, I rely on the stereotype. It makes life so much easier. I told Barbara not to worry about it, because after thirty years of being out, I'm used to people wrongly assuming I'm straight. But that doesn't make the mistake okay. I don't think Barbara was homophobic. Barbara presumed, based on heteronormative information: man's voice, plus married, equals wife. Until I proved her wrong.

In part, I felt like I had led her astray. I had used a gender-neutral term instead of a gender-specific term. I said "spouse" instead of "husband." Had I said "husband," Barbara likely would've said, "What's your husband's name?" At that moment, I started referring to Mike as my husband at all times, instead of my spouse—to make it crystal clear that I am not straight.

But that's how life works. Straight and cisgender until proved otherwise. And yes, I'm in a same-name relationship.

So why do LGBTQ2+ people have to come out? Technically, we don't *have* to come out. I mean, I don't come out to every taxi driver I encounter. There's no phaser set to glitter pointed at my head. But I believe it's important for LGBTQ2+ people to come out for two specific reasons.

First, coming out is about self-respect. There is still a huge amount of stigma and shame that accompanies being LGBTQ2+. The vast majority of LGBTQ2+ people struggle because we live in a world that regularly reminds us that being LGBTQ2+ is somehow not "normal." The world is built around hetero, cis categorizations that children are subjected to at an early age: boys like blue and girls like pink. Have you ever been to a so-called gender reveal party (that hopefully didn't cause a massive wildfire) where the confetti was anything other than blue or pink?

Consider Ed Smart, father of famous kidnapping victim Elizabeth Smart. In 2019, at the age of sixty-four, he came out as gay after struggling to accept his sexual orientation for his entire life. Smart, a member of the Church of Jesus Christ of Latter-Day Saints, said in an interview with *CBS This Morning*, "I was praying that I was not [gay]. I didn't want to believe that I was."[1]

Smart's case is just one of millions of examples of the shame that LGBTQ2+ people feel when reckoning with their identity. But people must be able to speak their truth and let go of their shame, so they can live healthy, productive lives. (Did I seriously just say "speak their truth"? Who am I? Dr. Phil?) Straight, cisgender people can help with this by creating safe spaces for LGBTQ2+ people so that coming out doesn't feel like a risk.

Second, coming out is important because people pay a high price for hiding parts of themselves, especially from anyone they have substantive interactions with. If I hide my identity, I don't have as connected a relationship with another person. On top of that, coming out to some people is necessary in order to facilitate the relationship, as I'll explain in a minute. In any case, I have to go through the mental calisthenics of deciding whether or not I'm going to show my cards to each person I meet. Not once, but every day of my life, I have to ask myself a series of questions.

First, I have to decide if it matters if I come out to this person. Taxi driver: no. My accountant: yes. No offense to taxi drivers, but their work is transactional. I get into the car, the driver takes me from point A to point B, and I spend the entire time scrolling through pictures of cats on Instagram. My accountant is a different story. That is a far more interactive relationship. They'll need to know my marital status and whether I have any dependents. The name of my spouse is Mike. Generally, that gives people some idea of what's going on.

Next, I have to ask myself, is coming out going to impact the relationship? Is it integral information? Again, with a taxi driver, no. He doesn't need to know anything about my personal life. My accountant, they absolutely do.

Lastly, I need to think about what I'll do if the response isn't positive. What happens if I tell my accountant that my spouse is a man, and they react negatively? In Canada there are protections, in that you can't deny someone services because of, among other things, their sexual orientation or gender identity or expression. That's not so in the United States, nor in other parts of the world. So, I need to consider the potential reaction. And it is not out of the realm of possibility that a person would react negatively. Consider the case of Charlie Craig and David Mullins v. Masterpiece Cakeshop of Lakewood, Colorado. Charlie and David wanted a cake for their wedding, but the owners of Masterpiece Cakeshop declined to make it because they didn't believe in same-sex marriage. Eventually, the case went to the US Supreme Court, where the court ruled in favor of the homophobic bakers.[2] That is the reality that LGBTQ2+ folks face in every interaction. It could go well, or we might get refused service—or the exchange could even turn violent, as it does every day.

Now apply all this to interactions with colleagues. Or neighbors. Or fellow congregants. Or an economics professor. Or anyone else a person has regular interaction with. Does someone need to know that I'm gay? That depends if I want to be fully engaged in my relationship or if I want to spend a lot of time changing pronouns, or simply not talking about my personal life.

Generally, most people don't compartmentalize at work. Coworkers can become friends (or enemies . . . or frenemies), even if that's only the case during working hours. The first thing that people ask on Monday morning is, "How was your weekend?" If I'm not "out," I can use a lot of mental and emotional energy trying to ensure that my coworkers don't discover that my husband and I went to the garden center and got our stunning backyard ready for our ever-loved annual pride party. (Hypothetically, of course. It is stunning, but I don't like people enough to have a pride party.)

Now imagine doing that with your parents; your extended family; your friends; the people at the dog park; the people in your spin class; the people you volunteer with; and so on, and so on. Every day, in every moment, LGBTQ2+ people have to decide whether to come out.

I still deliberately use the term "husband" when I refer to Mike. First, because he *is* my husband. We are legally wed. When the minister said, "I now pronounce you..." the word "wife" didn't come up. I also use it is because it implies my sexual orientation and gender identity. The term "husband" conjures another set of assumptions—that I'm a cisgender gay man. I may or may not be. I could be bisexual, pansexual, demisexual. I could be genderqueer or non-binary. But I've learned to accept those assumptions, because the alternative of being assumed straight and cis is at best annoying and at worst offensive.

Nothing against straight cis people. Some of my closest friends are straight and cis. But I'm a proud member of the LGBTQ2+ communities. It annoys me that people assume. After fifty years of such assumptions, it gets a little exhausting to have to continually correct people.

Give It a Try

I'd now like to invite you to put yourself in the shoes of an LGBTQ2+ person by completing my adaptation of the Heterosexual Questionnaire.[3]

Martin Rochlin was a scholar, activist, and pioneer in the field of gay-affirmative psychotherapy. His efforts led to the removal of homosexuality from the list of mental disorders in the *Diagnostic and Statistical Manual of Mental Disorders*. In 1972, he created the Heterosexual Questionnaire with the goal of helping straight (and presumably cisgender) people understand what LGBTQ2+ people go through on a regular basis.

Give it a try. Answer the following questions as honestly as possible. You may find it hard—that's kinda the point.

1 What do you think caused your heterosexuality?

2 When and how did you first decide you were cisgender?

3 To whom have you disclosed your heterosexual tendencies? How did they react?

4 Is it possible that your heterosexuality stems from a neurotic fear of others of the same sex?

5 Is it possible that your cisgender identity is just a phase you may grow out of?

6 Do you think you may have turned to heterosexuality out of fear of rejection?

7 If you've never had sex with a person of the same sex, how do you know that you wouldn't prefer that?

8 Why do you straight people feel compelled to seduce others into your sexual orientation?

9 If you should choose to nurture children, would you want them to be cisgender, knowing the problems they would face?

10 The great majority of child molesters are heterosexuals. Do you consider it safe to expose your children to heterosexual teachers?

11 Why do you insist on being so obvious, and making a public spectacle of your cisgender identity? Can't you just be who you are and keep it quiet?

12 Heterosexuals are noted for assigning themselves and one another narrowly restricted, stereotyped sex roles. Why do you cling to such unhealthy role-play?

13 How can you enjoy a fully satisfying sexual experience or deep emotional rapport with a person of the opposite sex, when the obvious biological and temperamental differences between you are so vast? How can a man understand what pleases a woman sexually, or vice versa?

14 Even with all the societal support marriage receives, the divorce rate is spiraling. Why are there so few stable relationships among heterosexuals?

15 There seem to be very few happy cisgender people. Techniques have been developed with which you might be able to change if you really want to. Have you considered trying aversion therapy?

16 Do heterosexuals hate or distrust others of the same sex? Is that what makes them heterosexual?

17 Could you really trust a cisgender therapist to be objective and unbiased? Don't you fear they might be inclined to influence you in the direction of their own feelings?

If you really took that questionnaire seriously, you'd probably be feeling something between shame, anger, and sadness—or all of the above. LGBTQ2+ folks face these questions all the time. Not just in the 1970s, but in the 2020s. Now you know what it feels like.

The moral of this story is this: Although LGBTQ2+ people have come a long way toward inclusion, a litany of homophobic, transphobic, and biphobic acts still occur every day. It's important for you to know that this happens—and to believe it happens. Just because you don't witness it doesn't mean it isn't happening.

Our goal now should be to create spaces where LGBTQ2+ people can choose to come out because you've shown them that they will be safe to do so.

Key Takeaways

- People will assume that you are straight and cisgender until you correct them.

- Coming out doesn't happen once. It happens every day, with every new person you encounter.

- When you assume you know a person's gender, you make an ass out of you. (You don't make an ass out of me. I do that all on my own.)

5

THE IMPORTANCE OF SAFE SPACE

I am proud, that

I found the courage to deal

the initial blow to the hydra

of public contempt.

KARL HEINRICH ULRICHS, born in Germany
in 1825 and known as one of the first gay men
to publicly announce his sexual orientation

would be remiss if I didn't include a chapter on safe space (sometimes interchangeably called positive space). It is, after all, fundamental to the entire conversation of LGBTQ2+ inclusion.

Let's start with a definition. Merriam-Webster defines safe space as "a place (as on a college campus) intended to be free of bias, conflict, criticism, or potentially threatening actions, ideas, or conversations."[1]

Including the reference to college campuses in the definition is somewhat accurate in that safe spaces have become commonplace in the academic world. But according to author Moira Rachel Kenney, in her book *Mapping Gay L.A.*, the concept of safe space stems from gay and lesbian bars in the mid-1960s. This was a time when being LGBTQ2+ was illegal in most parts of the world, and bars became a respite from the potential violence and oppression that people faced outside those safe spaces. The women's movement of the 1960s took the concept even further. I'll let Dr. Kenney explain it:

Safety and safe spaces, however, are about more than free-dom from crime and harassment (police or otherwise). As developed in the context of the women's movement, the notion of safe space implies a certain license to speak and act freely, form collective strength, and generate strat-egies for resistance. Although bars represent one type of space—a momentary respite from oppression—the wom-en's movement sought to create a radically different sort of place, one where the energy and collective effort to create place were the defining features. Safe space, in the wom-en's movement, was a means rather than an end and not only a physical space but also a space created by the coming together of women searching for community.[2]

In simpler terms, a safe space is one where people can be safe, in every way, and where they can be themselves.

Certain people have mocked the concept of safe space as one that coddles those who are overly sensitive and unpre-pared for the real world. These are the type of people who would tell their son to "man up." Richard Dawkins is a UK-based evolutionary biologist and writer who tweeted, "A university is not a 'safe space.' If you need a safe space, leave, go home, hug your teddy & suck your thumb until ready for university."[3] Spoken as a presumably straight, white, able-bodied man who one imagines has never faced a moment of discrimination in his privileged life.

When I think about safe space, I'm immediately drawn to the premise of safety. The world is not a safe place when you don't fit into a certain box. This concept is difficult to understand if you are in the majority. Most women who have been sexualized or objectified, or who have otherwise been the target of sexism, understand it. Most people of color understand it, having experienced subtle or overt acts of racism. Most people with disabilities understand it, having been forced to navigate a world that is designed for the able-bodied. And most LGBTQ2+ people understand it, because even if they have never personally experienced violence or discrimination because of their sexual or gender diversity, they've certainly witnessed it.

Many people, particularly those who are straight and cisgender, think violence against LGBTQ2+ people is no longer an issue. A 2015 report by the Canadian Centre for Diversity and Inclusion called *In & Out: Diverging Perspectives on LGBT Inclusion in the Workplace* found that 67.2 percent of straight cisgender respondents said there was no discrimination against LGBTQ2+ people. Conversely, 62.3 percent of the LGBTQ2+ respondents said they had either witnessed or experienced discrimination.[4]

That's not a dig at straight cis people. It's just not their reality. And believing in something that you've never experienced is difficult. Like a unicorn. You've never seen one, but they totally exist. When you see power queers like Ellen DeGeneres and Laverne Cox, you might not readily accept that LGBTQ2+ people still face violence and discrimination. But we do. And not in small numbers. And not in the past. Today. Let me remind you of these sobering statistics:

- Seventy-one countries in the world criminalize private, consensual, same-sex sexual activities.[5]

- In eleven of those countries, the potential punishment is death.[6]

- In fifteen countries, it is illegal to be Trans* or gender diverse.[7]

Now you might be thinking, yeah, but that's places like Turkmenistan and Brunei. Who even knows if those places actually exist? As long as LGBTQ2+ people don't go there, it's all good. Right?

Wrong. There is a long list of homophobic, transphobic, and biphobic acts that have been committed in places like Australia, Canada, the United Kingdom, and the United States, every day. Try these on for size:

- Seaman August Provost was found shot to death and his body burned at his guard post on Camp Pendleton on June 30, 2009. Provost had been harassed because of his sexual orientation.[8]

- CeCe McDonald, an African American Trans* woman, was attacked outside a bar late at night on June 5, 2011, in Minneapolis, Minnesota. CeCe fatally stabbed her attacker with a pair of scissors. She was subsequently convicted of manslaughter and jailed for nineteen months in a men's prison.[9]

- On October 12, 2013, Scott Jones, a gay man from New Glasgow, Nova Scotia, was stabbed by a man after leaving a bar. The attacker made homophobic comments before and during the attack.[10]

- On June 12, 2016, Omar Mateen, a twenty-nine-year-old security guard, killed forty-nine people and wounded fifty-three others in a mass shooting inside the Pulse nightclub in Orlando, Florida. While Mateen claimed that his actions were in retaliation to the United States air strikes in Iraq and Syria, it has been suspected that Mateen was gay and deeply closeted. Regardless, Mateen specifically targeted the nightclub because of its patrons.[11]

- On November 22, 2016, Tyrone Unsworth, from Brisbane, Australia, committed suicide after years of bullying related to his sexual orientation. Unsworth was thirteen.[12]

- In 2019, a lesbian couple in London, England, were harassed and assaulted during the early morning of May 30, while riding the bus. Reportedly, four teenagers (ages fifteen to eighteen) began harassing the pair after discovering they were a couple, asking them to kiss, making sexual gestures, discussing sex positions, and throwing coins. The situation escalated, and both women were significantly beaten.[13]

- On August 28, 2020, three men in their early twenties were charged with assault in Orillia, Ontario, after they hurled homophobic slurs and physically assaulted a gay man who was holding his boyfriend's hand while walking down the street. [14]

- At least 350 Trans* and non-binary people were killed in 2020. That vast majority were people of color.[15] If that statistic isn't sobering, I can't imagine what is.

I could go on... and on, and on, and on. But I think you get the point. The truth of the matter is that LGBTQ2+ people can face violence and discrimination at any time, in any place. Marriage equality didn't magically erase homophobia, transphobia, and biphobia. It just means that your in-laws can't take your stuff when your spouse dies.

The vast majority of LGBTQ2+ people live with a heightened sense of insecurity because they don't know what is lurking around the corner. Because of that reality, we need to create safe spaces where people can go and not face discrimination because of who they are.

How to Create Safe Space

Let's look specifically at how you create safe space. First, it's important to note that we are not necessarily talking about an actual physical space. I am not asking you to create a little office where people can watch *RuPaul's Drag Race* and scream, "Yaaasss, qween!" The point is to ensure that every part of your space—whether that's an office, a place of worship, a classroom, a digital forum, or something else—is safe. This has been a bit of a sticking point for me about safe-space programs on campuses. I just heard some academic gasps. Hold on for a second and hear me out.

My mother, Karen, was the campus chaplain at a university for ten years. Every time I visited her, I'd note the safe-space sticker on the door of her office; it featured an inverted triangle filled with the LGBTQ2+ rainbow flag colors and the words "Lesbian, Gay, Bisexual, Transgender, Queer Positive Space" emblazoned on it. Mom was really proud of it. She wanted students to know that they could be themselves in her presence.

Every so often, it would be defaced by some knuckle dragger who thought he (and you know it was probably a "he") was being funny or was just a total homophobe, and Mom would always replace it as quickly as possible. (Knowing her, I'm sure she had a box of the stickers in her desk drawer.)

But the sticker wasn't on the door of every office and classroom. Some staff and faculty didn't agree with it and refused to put it up. What message do LGBTQ2+ people get in that instance? Over here in this space, it's safe—but it may or may not be safe over there, and since there's no sticker, you have to guess. I worry that this guessing game is confusing for LGBTQ2+ people, especially students, who may suddenly find themselves facing discrimination and violence because they thought it was a safe space, but it turns out they were in the wrong room on campus.

The point is that safe space is more of a mindset and a culture than it is a physical space. And although you may never get everyone to buy in, you do need the majority to drink the Kool-Aid.

So, let's break down the building blocks of safe space and provide you with a road map to ensure your space will be safe for LGBTQ2+ people.

Policies and Procedures

In employment settings, a review of policies and procedures is traditionally part of something called an Employment Systems Review, or ESR. This practice can be applied easily in organizations such as churches, community centers, and the like, through a simple analysis of systems and policies as they relate to employees and the communities served. Traditionally an ESR is conducted as part of a compliance exercise, but it has become more commonplace in organizations that want to understand where there may be barriers to inclusion. The purpose of an ESR is fivefold:

1   to identify all your human resources systems, policies, and practices;

2   to analyze these systems, policies, and practices to determine how they may have a different impact on designated group members compared to those who are not members of a designated group;

3   to identify which of these systems, policies, and practices create barriers;

4   to provide a basis for corrective action to remove barriers; and

5   to assess the potential for reasonable accommodation to overcome valid barriers (in other words, barriers that exist because of a bona fide occupational requirement and are consistent with human rights legislation).[16]

First and foremost, your policies and procedures need to be inclusive. Start by reviewing your policies to ensure that people aren't inadvertently being excluded. For example, consider your parental leave policy. Is it called a "parental leave policy" or a "maternity leave policy"? If the latter, I'd invite you to join the rest of us in the twenty-first century and start with a name change. "Maternity leave" is a term entrenched in law that speaks to leave provided to a person who has a child through biological means. Parental leave is not just about biological females having kids. Not only are men involved in the process of making babies (it's true ... I looked it up on Wikipedia), but there are also lots of different variations of "parent."

I recall one employer I was working with that had some (at the time) forward-thinking policies around parenting, including benefits for those who adopted or used surrogates. But they had never considered LGBTQ2+ parents, and they were trying to decide if they should extend the surrogate benefit to a same-sex couple. You can imagine how that couple felt. Talk about sending the wrong message. The employer asked me if they should make an *exception* and extend the benefit. I seem to recall that my reaction was, "Don't be f$#&ing ridiculous. Extend the benefit, and don't make it an exception—make it the rule!" A policy for one is a policy for all, or it becomes what I like to call "discrimination."

The key is to ensure that your policies are applied equitably and that you aren't deliberately or inadvertently leaving anyone out. As an example, if you're a volunteer-run organization, you should be open to all volunteers, regardless of their sexuality or gender. A youth mentorship organization that I know of advertises itself as being inclusive of LGBTQ2+ youth,[17] but what about their volunteers? If I were a Trans* woman, would I be able to volunteer and be matched with a kid in need? And would that kid be a girl? Would they match me with only Trans*-identified kids? Why would it matter? If you have a kid in need, wouldn't having them mentored by a Trans* woman be just as helpful as a woman who was assigned female at birth? There are definitely some exceptions to this—like a rape crisis center that hires only women—but those exceptions are few and far between. Or at least they should be.

Once you've reviewed your policies, it's time to review your procedures. Policies are one thing, but they're only as valuable as the digital paper they're printed on if they're not followed exactly as intended. And they're not. They never are. We all know of people who don't follow policy to the letter. The ideal state is to enforce policies exactly as they're written to ensure people aren't taking liberties. But that's probably not realistic. A policy police officer is not going to monitor every situation to make sure the policy is applied exactly as intended. Aside from that, anticipating every scenario in which the policy will need to be interpreted is next to impossible.

But consider your recruiting process as an example: Do you have a set list of questions that you ask all candidates, or do you allow hiring managers to make up their own questions? If the latter, you may find them asking questions like, "I see you're wearing a wedding band. What does your [opposite sex spouse] do?"

Consistency is key. Make sure that all your procedures run as intended and that they aren't exclusionary of LGBTQ2+ people, either inadvertently or, worse, deliberately.

Language

Language is a tricky one. We're often stuck in the words we use, and changing old habits is hard. However, the language you use can be a sign of whether or not you provide a safe space for LGBTQ2+ folks. I recall an employer I began to work for (admittedly this was decades ago), and when I looked through their HR policies, and specifically their code of conduct, there was no mention of sexual orientation or gender identity and expression anywhere. That sent a message to me: LGBTQ2+ people weren't being thought of as part of the organization, or at the very least, they were an afterthought.

Many LGBTQ2+ people are experts at reading between the lines. If a Trans* person with passing privilege reads language like "he/she" in organizational policies and documentation, they (as a gender fabulous person) might sense they would not be as welcome if they came out.

Changing language can seem like such a simple thing to do, but it can be quite difficult because we are so programmed to think in the binary. Everywhere we turn we see it: restrooms, toys, clothing, classes. So much is built around the concept of two data points: man and woman.

Ensure the language you use in policies and statements is explicit. The terms are "sexual orientation" and "gender identity and expression." Go further to use gender-neutral language. Use terms like "partner" or "spouse" instead of "husband" and "wife." Instead of he/she, use they or them. It may seem like you're speaking in the third person and finally slipping into the abyss of madness that you always knew would consume you, but it's inclusive. And please see a doctor about that other thing.

One more great example of changing the tone is to include personal pronouns in email signatures. My personal pronouns are he/him, and they appear in every email I send out. And to look at me, most would assume that is how I identify. But you don't know that for sure. Including personal pronouns in an email signature removes the guessing and misgendering. It also takes the onus off Trans* and non-binary folks to educate cisgender people, which isn't their job.

Terms to Avoid

Keeping in mind that language can be an indicator for people, there are a few terms you will want to avoid on your journey to being LGBTQ2+ inclusive.

Normal. Being straight and/or cisgender doesn't make you "normal." It makes you common. There are simply more straight cisgender people in the world than there are LGBTQ2+ people. Generally speaking, I'd suggest you dump this word altogether. It's problematic in so many ways.

Gay. If you're referring to my sexual orientation, you can use the term "gay." I am gay. But using phrases like "gay village" or "gay pride" is not inclusive of the many members of the LGBTQ2+ communities that are part of the bigger picture. It's LGBTQ2+ pride and the LGBTQ2+ village. Further, saying things like, "That's so gay!" is so 1998. It wasn't a compliment then and it's not a compliment now.

Lifestyle/lifestyle choices. Being LGBTQ2+ is not a lifestyle choice. Living in a gated community is a lifestyle choice. I didn't get to choose being gay, so please stop suggesting I did.

Sexual preference. This one is a bit questionable. Although it's true I have a preference (*j'aime the mens*), saying "preference" suggests that I have a choice in the matter. It's also not consistent for some people. People who are bisexual or pansexual might not have a preference.

Education

Once you've reviewed policies and procedures, the next critical step is to educate your people—that means employees, volunteers, and community members. Just rewriting a policy isn't going to change hearts and minds. You must educate them through in-person workshops, eLearning, guest speakers, and all the other forms of education. What is LGBTQ2+ inclusion? Why does it matter? What does it mean for me as an individual?

For some, the concept of being inclusive of LGBTQ2+ people is easy. They have a gay BFF, a lesbian sister, a Trans* cousin. Easy-peasy lemon-drop martini. These are allies—people who are straight and/or cisgender and are actively advocating for LGBTQ2+ inclusion.

For some others, those who perhaps don't have an openly LGBTQ2+ person in their life, inclusion may be a challenging concept. You'll note I said *openly* LGBTQ2+ person, because these people likely have someone in their life who is LGBTQ2+ but because they don't know if it is safe to come out, they choose to stay in the closet.

I think the concept of inclusion is hardest for armchair allies to grasp. I describe an armchair ally as someone who isn't homophobic, transphobic, or biphobic, but they're also not playing an active role in LGBTQ2+ inclusion. They're a bit of a passive bystander. These are the people who, when they hear a joke with an LGBTQ2+ person as the punchline, don't say anything. They're supportive, but they're not in the trenches, fighting the fight. These are the people who think being an ally is not getting offended when they see nudity at their local pride festival.

Any organization is likely to have three different stakeholder groups—armchair allies, active allies, and everyone else—and each group will have varying degrees of understanding of the concepts of LGBTQ2+ inclusion. Worst of all, you can't tell them apart. So, you must educate all your people—because each has a role in creating an LGBTQ2+ inclusive environment.

Training Safe-Space Champions

I have separated education from training because I want to talk about a leading practice: safe-space champions.

I first came across this many years ago when the Ontario Public Service Pride Network created their Positive Space Champions program. Their objective was to create an inclusive public service with respect to LGBTQ2+ issues in the workplace. The idea was to take the concept of positive space, and instead of hanging a sticker and being done, you had to take a six-part eLearning course and an interactive webinar before you could graduate and call yourself a Positive Space Champion.[18]

What I love about the Positive Space Champions program is that it moves beyond policy and education to practical lived experience. It requires an answer to the question: What are you going to do to ensure (the OPS) is an inclusive place for LGBTQ2+ people?

This is an excellent leading practice that all organizations should adopt to ensure that your armchair allies become active allies. All your people—employees, volunteers, faculty, health care providers, and so on—should understand their role in creating an LGBTQ2+ inclusive space. An offering such as this is a quick win and sends such a strong message.

Zero Tolerance

I have to include zero tolerance here, because everyone says they have a zero-tolerance policy when it comes to their Code of Conduct. But they don't. They are what I like to call "full of it." Even organizations with written zero-tolerance policies often bypass them in situations where someone is deemed to be a "high performer."

One employer I worked with was so proud of their zero-tolerance policy, or what they called their "no jerk" rule. It was simple: don't be a jerk or you're out. And yet if I had a nickel for every time I saw behavior that would politely be called *jerkesque* conduct and there was absolutely no consequence, I would have a truckload of nickels. And I'm talking a dump truck, not a four-by-four. And I was a consultant, so I can only imagine what was happening when I wasn't in the room.

Here's the truth: If you say you have a zero-tolerance policy, you have to enforce it. The first time you don't, you completely devalue the policy, and no one will ever believe you again.

If you ever hear someone say, "But they're such a high performer!" when referring to someone who is being homophobic/transphobic/biphobic/sexist/racist/*whateverist*, ask yourself: Does the revenue they bring in outweigh how much they cost you?

Consider this: In 2017, a Work Institute study showed that it costs employers 33 percent of an employee's salary to hire a replacement if that worker leaves.[19] Other studies have shown similar calculations, but the higher up a person is in the organization, the more it costs. For example, the cost to replace a $100,000 CEO is $213,000—or 213 percent of their salary.[20] Those costs appear in the time and resources it takes to post the job, review résumés, conduct phone screenings and interviews, and negotiate an offer. That's all before the person starts. Then there's the expense of getting the person up to speed to do the job. All in all, it's a pretty penny.

Then consider the cost of lower levels of engagement, increased training, lack of productivity, human rights complaints, and legal action. Remind me again how much of a rainmaker that person is? If you run the numbers, you might find that the bad apple *is* actually spoiling the bunch.

Zero-tolerance policies work because they set a tone. It doesn't change people's belief systems, but it does set expectations and it does change behavior, which in itself is a win. *If* the policies are enforced. There is a caveat to this, which we'll talk about in chapter 8.

Symbolism

I mention the idea of symbolism with a forewarning: you can't use it in isolation. Years ago, the LGBTQ2+ Employee Resource Group (ERG) at one employer I was working with decided they were going to do a safe-space campaign and they were going to distribute rainbow stickers that people could put up at their desks to indicate that they were allies of LGBTQ2+ people.

Their first mistake was that they did it in isolation: no one in leadership knew about it; they didn't provide any education about the expected behavior of the people who had the stickers at their desks; there was no policy or procedure review to know if there were unintended barriers; they didn't have a zero-tolerance policy; and there was no real recourse to deal with homophobic, transphobic, or biphobic behavior. And... 💥

It got ugly, to say the least. The ERG had to remove all the stickers, and they subsequently put their tail between their legs and weren't heard from for quite some time.

Symbolism is important. When I go into an organization, I look for some little sign that tells me it's a safe place: a rainbow flag; a pink triangle; something/anything that says I am going to be welcome for who I am. If you're going to do a campaign that focuses on the visual, then you have to do it in conjunction with other steps to make sure it doesn't blow up in your face:

- Involve leadership.
- Educate people about expected behaviors.
- Review policies and procedures.
- Enact a zero-tolerance policy and hold people accountable.

To be clear, I do encourage you to run a visual campaign because it sends an extraordinarily strong message. If I see a rainbow flag on the door of a Starbucks, it's a pretty safe assumption that my husband and I are going to be welcome there. That's not to say I wouldn't be welcome if there wasn't a rainbow flag, but without it, I'm left guessing. Can my husband and I hold hands, or is someone going to make a homophobic comment while they're preparing my grande almond no-water chai latte? A sign doesn't guarantee my safety, but it is a good indicator.

Now that you know that, consider using a visual to send a message of inclusion. Remember that LGBTQ2+ folks tend to be the invisible minority, so until we see something that tells us we're welcome, we may continue to hide.

The pink triangle dates back to Nazi Germany and was used in concentration camps to identify gay men. Homosexuality was made illegal in Germany in 1871, but the law was rarely enforced, until the Nazi Party took power in 1933.

In Hitler's effort to "purify" Germany, the Nazis arrested upward of one hundred thousand LGBTQ2+ individuals (mostly gay men), and somewhere between five thousand and fifteen thousand were placed in concentration camps. Just as Jews were forced to identify themselves with a yellow star, gay men had to wear a large pink triangle.[21] It wasn't until October of 1973, when Germany's first gay rights organization, Homosexuelle Aktion Westberlin (HAW), reclaimed the pink triangle as a symbol of liberation, that it began to be adopted by LGBTQ2+ rights organization around the world.[22]

The rainbow flag came about in 1978 when artist Gilbert Baker, an openly gay man, designed the first version of the rainbow flag, at the urging of Harvey Milk, a civil rights activist and the first openly gay elected official in the United States. Milk wanted Baker to create a symbol of pride for the LGBTQ2+ communities to rally behind. Baker chose the flag because he saw flags as powerful symbols of pride, such as the American flag. The original design included eight colors, each with its own meaning (hot pink for sex, red for life, orange for healing, yellow for sunlight, green for nature, turquoise for art, indigo for harmony, and violet for spirit). When it came to mass production, the pink and turquoise weren't readily available, and the indigo was replaced by basic blue.[23]

In 2018, designer Daniel Quasar rebooted the rainbow flag with the goal of making it more inclusive. Quasar added black and brown stripes to represent people of color, and baby blue, pink, and white to represent the inclusion of Trans* and non-binary folks.[24] This new flag is being widely adopted, as people feel it is more inclusive of the broader diversity within the LGBTQ2+ communities.

Whichever symbol you choose, you can use it in a variety of means, including hanging a rainbow flag in a public space, posting the pink triangle on your organization's intranet, or changing your company logo for Pride Month to include the rainbow colors. All of these are signs for LGBTQ2+ folks that yours is a safe space.

Let's Celebrate Good Times

Ugh. Now I have "Celebration" by Kool & the Gang going through my head. Stupid earworm!

Celebrations are a bold sign of LGBTQ2+ inclusion. If you're hosting an LGBTQ2+ pride celebration in your office, church, school, and so on, you're sending a strong signal that it's an LGBTQ2+ inclusive space. The thing to remember is... I'm going to be gay in October. And November. And pretty much every day of the year.

I will fully admit that keeping up with everything you could and should be celebrating can be demanding. There are some important dates on the calendar: Black History Month, International Women's Day, National Indigenous History Month, National Chocolate Pudding Day, and *sooo* many more.

Because of that, and in an attempt to keep your LGBTQ2+ inclusion work top of mind, I suggest moving your celebrations away from June. Although June is officially Pride Month in the United States and Canada, there are pride festivals that start as early as April and go as late as November—and that's just on one continent. Pride Month is going to happen even if you don't have a pride event with rainbow-colored cupcakes. (Why is it always rainbow-colored cupcakes?! Don't people understand that the gays don't eat carbs for at least three months prior to Pride?)

For example, the International Transgender Day of Visibility is March 31. International Day Against Homophobia, Transphobia and Biphobia (IDAHOBIT) is May 17. National Coming Out Day is October 11. These are arguably just as important as LGBTQ2+ Pride Month and also present a great opportunity to educate people. Spread the love across the calendar and use these events as educational opportunities to help people understand the reality faced by LGBTQ2+ folks and the need for inclusion.

Nothing about Us without Us

Good intention is nice. But it can also tank what you're trying to achieve. There are so many examples of this that it's hard to pick just one . . . but I will: the treatment of Indigenous people.

For years, white people have been deciding what's good for Indigenous people. One only has to look at Canada's history of residential schools as an example. If you're not familiar, I invite you to ask Google. So many people had not given much thought (if they even knew about them) to these church- and government-run schools until the spring of 2021, when 215 children (some as young as three) were found in an unmarked grave. And that's just one of over 130 schools. Many countries beyond Canada, particularly those that have been colonized, have long, unfortunate histories with Indigenous peoples. But we know better! Right?

Wrong. The concept of "nothing about us without us" is a slogan used to describe the idea that no policy or action that affects a group should be taken without input from that group. And this is a perfect example.

If you're going to focus on LGBTQ2+ safe space, you must engage some of your LGBTQ2+ employees in designing what that program or initiative looks like. They're the ones living the reality. If you're straight and cisgender, you need to make room for your LGBTQ2+ colleagues to have a voice in the work.

That's not to say that straight cis people can't be involved. It's to say that to ensure you have included a variety of perspectives, you need to actually include a variety of perspectives.

Safe Space for All

I forgot to mention one little secret: safe space for LGBTQ2+ people is safe space for all. That's right. We're willing to share! How awesome are we?!

When you think about safe space, consider that there are lots of people who face discrimination in your organization. I'm not suggesting that the experiences of a white cisgender woman are similar to that of a Trans* woman of color. That's a round of the Oppression Olympics (where groups compete to see who is the most mistreated) that I'm not going to step into.

That said, if you want to create a safe-space initiative, consider an approach that is inclusive of all people. Focus on the elimination of all of the isms—those that impact women, people of color, people with disabilities, immigrants, religious minorities, Indigenous people, *and* LGBTQ2+ people. Don't leave anyone outside the tent. If you're smart, you'll be able to devise a strategy that takes everyone into consideration and creates an inclusive space for all people.

The most successful version I have seen of this is in a health care organization I had the opportunity to work with. In creating a safe-space program, they wanted to be sure that it was inclusive of all people. Although the initiative was being driven by the organization's LGBTQ2+ Employee Resource Group, the members of the group recognized that applying an intersectional lens would ensure they were being inclusive not only of all LGBTQ2+ people, but of everyone in their organization—patients, medical staff, support staff, volunteers, and suppliers—regardless of each person's unique identities. Safe space for one is safe space for all.

Put a Bow on It

If you haven't figured it out yet, creating a safe space is the work you need to do to make sure your organization is inclusive. It's the foundation to successfully generating an environment where LGBTQ2+ people want to engage because it's a "safe" place (did a 💡 just go on?).

No one wants to go to work and feel unsafe. No one wants to volunteer in a place where they could face violence or discrimination because of who they are. No one wants to feel like they don't belong in their temple or school.

You will attract and retain LGBTQ2+ people (as employees, customers, volunteers, patients, and so on) if you first make sure yours is a safe space. If you don't know how, kindly reread this chapter and follow the steps. We'll wait for you to catch up.

Key Takeaways

- Safe space begins with a cultural mindset that all people are accepted, and that no one should, and no one does, fear discrimination for who they are.

- A safe-space initiative has multiple parts—policy and procedures, education, training, zero tolerance, and symbolism.

- Safe space for one should be safe space for all.

6

THE CASE FOR INCLUSIVE ORGANIZATIONS

Nature made

a mistake, which I

have corrected.

CHRISTINE JORGENSEN, one of the
first people to undergo gender
affirmation surgery and the first to
publicly speak about the process

thought I'd take a moment to answer the "why" question, as in, *why* should you be an active ally to LGBTQ2+ people, and *why* should organizations—from businesses to nonprofits to educational institutions to congregations to health care facilities and beyond—create LGBTQ2+ inclusive spaces?

I'm not going to speak about the legal aspect in this book. There are way too many potential legal frameworks for me to make a reasoned argument. But there is a business case to be made for employers, educators, clergy, and other community leaders to focus on LGBTQ2+ inclusion.

In the coming chapters, I refer to "employers" quite a bit. However, that word is meant to be interchangeable with others, like "church" or "monastery," "school," "college" or "university," "association," or "union." The information in this section is not exclusive to employers. It's just easier to say one thing and assume it refers to a bunch of other things. Because I'm really lazy.

The Cost of the Closet

Organizations don't think about how much it costs to *not* create inclusive space for LGBTQ2+ folks. But the price tag can be quite hefty. There's the cost of lower levels of engagement. The cost of higher levels of voluntary turnover. The cost of recruitment. The cost of decreased innovation. And just like when I enter a wine store, that bill can add up fast. So, how do you quantify the cost? I spent a lot of time trying to figure that out.

Then, around 2005, someone from IBM shared a model with me. The first time I saw it, I thought, "THIS! This is exactly what I've been trying to explain," and I used it to build a business case for why my employer needed an LGBTQ2+ Employee Resource Group.

The model is called "Will and Ned's Excellent Adventure." A guy named John Martin developed it after seeing the Broadway production of *Rent* on December 27, 1997.[1] With John's permission, I have reprinted a version of it on page 103. John describes what motivated him to create the model:

> I wanted a way to help people gain empathy for what it's like to hide an important part of yourself every day at work and to understand that coming out is not a one-time event. I knew this poster worked on a personal level when a straight person said, "I was exhausted just reading this. I can't imagine going through that every day." And I knew it worked on a business level when a straight ally, an IBM VP said, "This is the first thing I've seen that shows the cost to a business of having closeted employees." I used a flowchart to make

WILL AND NED'S EXCELLENT ADVENTURE!

What really happened this weekend: IBM employee Will and his life partner, Ned, celebrated 10 years together on Saturday. At 9:00 a.m., Will presented an envelope wrapped in anniversary paper to Ned... Inside, Ned found tickets to a show he has most wanted to see for years—*RENT*—on Broadway!

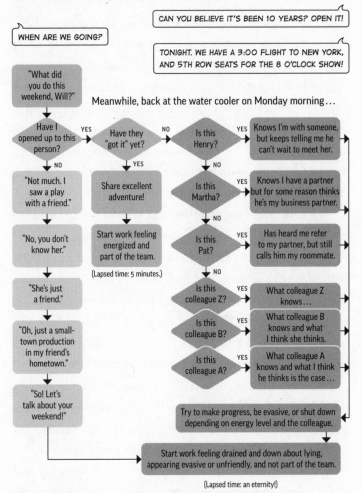

Meanwhile, back at the water cooler on Monday morning...

(Lapsed time: 5 minutes.)

(Lapsed time: an eternity!)

The Cost of the Closet

Lost Productivity | Reduced Teaming | Decreased Employee Morale

The average closeted LGBTQ2+ employee expends more energy by 9:00 a.m. answering the question, "What did you do this weekend?" than most employees expend all day.

CONCEPT BY JOHN MARTIN

the points because I knew a significant part of its audience at IBM was going to be programmers and engineers.[2]

"Will and Ned's Excellent Adventure" is a brilliant visual that shows just how complicated the answer to a simple water-cooler question can be for someone who is in the closet. What I love about it is that it illustrates, in detail, what every LGBTQ2+ person goes through daily. It is a visual model of the mental calisthenics that LGBTQ2+ folks have to perform with every new person they encounter—asking themselves a series of questions with layers of answers, in response to what might otherwise seem like innocuous chitchat.

Martin's model suggests that an LGBTQ2+ person in the closet spends an "eternity" trying to either educate people or be evasive. I worked for auditors and accountants for the better part of a decade, and they're not terribly comfortable with the number "eternity." So, I ran some numbers to try to quantify the cost of not providing an LGBTQ2+ inclusive space. Let's take a look at a hypothetical situation and put a price tag on it. Warning: there is about to be math.

Let's assume that an LGBTQ2+ person working for an organization that has not taken the time to ensure the workplace is LGBTQ2+ inclusive spends, on average, fifteen minutes of their day educating people or being evasive.

There are 480 minutes in an eight-hour workday and 124,800 minutes in a work year, give or take. Based on the original assumption, our LGBTQ2+ colleague spends 3,900 of those minutes either educating people on LGBTQ2+

inclusion (which likely isn't what they get paid to do) or masking their identity. Essentially, they waste sixty-five hours of their work year doing something that they shouldn't have to do—and their employer pays them for that time.

The average individual income in Canada is $51,272 (as of 2017[3]), and in the United States it's $48,516 (as of 2019[4]), so I'm going to use the median of $49,894. If an LGBTQ2+ person wastes 3,900 minutes because their workplace isn't LGBTQ2+ inclusive, that would mean $1,559.19 of their pay was wasted because they were doing something that they weren't getting paid for.

Let's assume that (a conservative) 5 percent of the population is LGBTQ2+. We have terrible data here because, to my knowledge, LGBTQ2+ identities have not traditionally been part of Census collection, but Gallup did a survey in 2017 that found that 4.5 percent of the US population identified as LGBTQ2+.[5] So, for the sake of argument, let's round up on this one.

Now let's assume that 20 percent of LGBTQ2+ people either are forced to be educators or are closeted at work. That's 1 percent of the workforce overall. Still with me?

The Canadian workforce amounts to 20,583,847 people (meaning there are that many people of "working age"— over sixteen and under sixty-five).[6] The United States is at 165,890,069.[7] Therefore, 1 percent of the Canadian workforce is 205,838, and in the United States it is 1,658,901.

So, if the math holds true and 205,838 people in Canada and 1,658,901 people in the United States are wasting

$1,559.19 of their pay by either being forced into the role of educator or being unable to be open about who they are... (drum roll please), employers in Canada are wasting $320,940,769.44 by not providing an LGBTQ2+ inclusive workplace, and US employers are wasting $2,586,537,219.59 for the same reason.

Even if you doubt my mathematical skills (which you should... my tenth-grade math teacher, Mrs. Love, can explain), the numbers don't lie. And these are conservative estimates. We know that more than 5 percent of the population is LGBTQ2+, but they are not self-identifying on surveys. We also know that the number of closeted LGBTQ2+ people is likely much higher than 1 percent. A study found that 48 percent of LGBTQ2+ employees do not come out at work.[8] We also know that $49,894 is an average, and there are a lot of people making a lot more.

Add it all up, and employers are wasting a huge amount of money by not creating spaces where LGBTQ2+ folks can bring their whole selves to work and do their jobs and be successful.

You can extrapolate this theory to show the potential cost in other environments as well. What if a hospital doesn't provide inclusive medical treatment for LGBTQ2+ people, and the hospital gets sued for malpractice? Or a faith-based organization loses donors because of its practices?

The Salvation Army is a Christian organization with a long history of doing good deeds for underprivileged individuals. And they have provided services to LGBTQ2+ people in need.[9] Yet, as recently as 2017, the Salvation Army of New York City was accused of refusing to provide service to Trans* folks at one of its substance abuse clinics.[10] In the past few decades, the Salvation Army has opposed same-sex marriage, refused to comply with LGBTQ2+ inclusive legislation, and fought against the repeal of anti-LGBT laws.[11]

Recently, a client asked my opinion about supporting a Salvation Army–run event because one of their LGBTQ2+ employees had raised concerns about supporting it, considering the Salvation Army's questionable relationship with the LGBTQ2+ communities. In discussions with the client, I asked if they would consider supporting an event that was patently unsafe. This client's business is safety, so the idea of sponsoring an event that ran counter to their core beliefs was, as I suspected, unfathomable. My question to them was simple: If diversity and inclusion is a strategic priority, then are you willing to support an organization that appears to work counter to that priority?

Now, I'm not saying that organizations should cut funding for the Salvation Army. They provide some important services. My point is that whenever your policies are out of line with potential funders, you risk losing fundraising income. Sponsorship is what allows organizations like the Salvation Army to do their good work. Losing a sponsor would impact their ability to deliver service, and if they couldn't deliver service, they would cease to exist. If they aren't willing to reexamine their practices and work to root out homophobia, transphobia, and biphobia in the organization, maybe they won't be around to ring the bell next Christmas.

We're Already Here

Face a fact: organizations already have LGBTQ2+ identified employees, students, clients, and community members. If your organization has ten or more people, statistically speaking there is a really good chance that people working for or with you identify as LGBTQ2+. If you don't know who they are yet, it is a good indicator that you need to work on creating a more inclusive space.

Do you have that one colleague who doesn't share much? They don't talk about what they did on the weekend. They never talk about having a significant other. They keep to themselves, for the most part. Yeah... that one. Those are not definitive indicators that a person is LGBTQ2+, but there's a chance.

Many LGBTQ2+ people are the invisible minority. Emphasis on *invisible*. Most LGBTQ2+ people don't have to come out, and arguably won't come out, until they know they are in a safe space. If you don't give them that signal, they'll quietly keep their heads down and stay in their closet—and they won't be as engaged or productive.

Engagement

The science on employee engagement is really sound. And ultimately pretty simple:

High Engagement = High Productivity = High Profitability

You don't have to be a rocket scientist to figure it out. If your employees are engaged, they will be more productive, and when your people are more productive, that leads to higher levels of profitability. (Or for those of you in the nonprofit space, it means you can do more with less... which is really just about productivity. You get the point. Stop harassing me. I'm feeling very attacked!)

If I can come to work and be myself—by having a picture of my husband on my desk and sharing what we did on the weekend—then I will be more open in the workplace, which ultimately leads to higher engagement in my work. I win, my employer wins.

Loyalty

With higher levels of engagement comes higher levels of loyalty. Many studies have looked at the impact of inclusion on LGBTQ2+ employees. In 2013, a group of researchers reviewed thirty-six studies and found that "LGBT-supportive policies and workplace climates are linked to greater job commitment, improved workplace relationships, increased job satisfaction, and improved health outcomes among LGBT employees. Furthermore, LGBT-supportive policies and workplace climates are also linked to less discrimination against LGBT employees and more openness about being LGBT. Less discrimination and more openness, in turn, are also linked to greater job commitment, improved workplace relationships, increased job satisfaction, improved health outcomes, and increased productivity among LGBT employees."[12]

More specifically, sixteen of those thirty-six studies found that LGBTQ2+ inclusive policies led to greater job commitment and had a positive business impact.

I could go on and on (but let's be honest, this chapter is getting a bit long). The point is that creating an LGBTQ2+ inclusive space means that your LGBTQ2+ employees, volunteers, students, or parishioners are going to be more loyal to your organization, which means a reduction in voluntary turnover rates and the costs related therein.

Key Takeaways

- Employers that do not create inclusive environments for their LGBTQ2+ employees pay significant costs.

- LGBTQ2+ inclusion leads to higher levels of engagement.

- LGBTQ2+ employees show significant loyalty to employers with inclusive, welcoming workplaces.

7

ATTRACTING LGBTQ2+ PEOPLE

Equality means more than passing laws. The struggle is really won in the hearts and minds of the community, where it really counts.

BARBARA GITTINGS, American activist

Before I proceed, let me be clear about this: do not start trying to attract LGBTQ2+ people into your organization before you've done the work to ensure your organization is inclusive, welcoming, and safe. *Don't* do it. You see how serious I am? I used italics!

If you do, you set yourself up for a significant kaboom. At the very least, you risk LGBTQ2+ people coming to your organization only to face homophobia, transphobia, and biphobia with no recourse to deal with it. At that point, they'll either (1) leave, (2) file a human rights complaint, or (3) sue you. Or a little bit of all three—all of which have a significant impact, either financial or reputational. So, if you skipped chapters 5 and 6, I strongly encourage you to go back and read them. And do the work. Consider yourself warned (insert "dun dun dunnn" sound effect here). Note to self: books should have sound effects.

Now that I've given you a big warning, and you've heeded my advice, done your homework, and built a solid foundation, you can turn your attention to how you can attract LGBTQ2+ people to your organization. Truthfully, attracting LGBTQ2+ people isn't all that different from attracting straight cisgender people. It just involves a lot more glitter and feather boas. I jest. Sort of.

This isn't a book on talent attraction. If you don't understand talent attraction models, I suggest you also read a book on talent attraction leading practices (not right now—finish this book first). What I have included in this chapter are a few considerations—things you should think about to attract LGBTQ2+ people into your organization. These are important points, but they're not the entire conversation.

One thing I'll say from the start is that you *must* do everything. You can't just pick and choose. Each point that I raise in the following pages is interconnected. Think of it like a chair. Each section is a leg of the chair. If you're missing a leg of a chair, what happens? That's right—you fall flat on your ass and people laugh at you, like in the movie *Carrie* (the original, not the remake). Don't be Carrie. This analogy is a bit off, but the important part is the chair. Not the Stephen King classic horror film. I'm going to move on now.

How Queer Is Your Brand?

Have you ever googled your organization name and "LGBTQ2"+ or any other version of the initialisms? Or what about searching your organization's intranet for these terms? Give it a try. I can wait. I need a refill of my wine anyway.

You may be wondering why, in a chapter on talent attraction, I'm including mention of brand. Simply put, your brand is what attracts potential employees, volunteers, patients, students, clients, and so on to you.

So, what did you find in your googling? Were you surprised? Was it upsetting? Was it confusing? I would wager you found one of three scenarios.

The Best-Case Scenario

The best-case scenario is that you discovered a really positive message. Maybe you're like Lexmark[1] and got a perfect score on the Corporate Equality Index from the Human Rights Campaign (HRC). That's a great news story. You can post that on your website and send out a press release and give everyone a rainbow-decorated cupcake (but not in June...carbs).

Or maybe you're like Boston Consulting Group, and your website includes specific content about your commitment to LGBTQ2+ inclusion.[2]

Either way, this is definitely a best-case scenario. An LGBTQ2+ person would look at these results and *infer* that your organization is one where they could bring their fabulous self and be welcomed (emphasis on "infer").

The Worst-Case Scenario

The worst-case scenario is that you found articles, blogs, or other content that present your organization in a negative light as it relates to LGBTQ2+ inclusion.

Maybe you're Altitude Express (Long Island, New York); Clayton County (Clayton County, Georgia); or R.G. & G.R. Harris Funeral Homes (Detroit, Michigan) and you were part of a lawsuit that was heard by the Supreme Court of the United States, which decided that an employer who fires an individual merely for being LGBTQ2+ violates Title VII of the Civil Rights Act of 1964.[3] Just try googling any of their names *without* "LGBTQ2+," and see how these companies are tarnished by these court cases.

Such a blemish on your brand endures. Consider the long boycott of Coors Beer by LGBTQ2+ bars around the world. In 1977, the Adolph Coors Beer company (Adolph: such a good name... that no one should ever give their child) had a clause in their employment contract requiring all employees to take a mandatory polygraph test in which they could be asked directly to reveal their sexual orientation. The union representing the workers called for a boycott, which led to a ban on Coors products being sold in LGBTQ2+ bars that lasted decades.[4]

The first time I went into an LGBTQ2+ bar (it was 1987 and I *may* have been underage), I moseyed up to the bar in my white Mexx turtleneck and navy blue brushed wool blazer (yes, the exact same outfit from a previous story—I loved that outfit), looked at the bartender, and asked for a Coors (because honestly, it was the only beer I could think of while in sheer terror that I was actually in an LGBTQ2+ bar). The smile vanished from his face, and he simply said, "We don't sell that shit here." It wasn't until Coors spent a lot of time and money rebuilding its relationship with the LGBTQ2+ communities that it got its suds back on the shelves of our bars.

PS: Why does it matter? Well, let me put it to you this way. Once upon a time, I researched and learned that of the top ten purchasers of beer in the City of Toronto, four of them were LGBTQ2+ establishments. That's right: the pink dollar is worth it! More on that later.

The Likely Scenario

The likely scenario is that if you googled your organization's name and "LGBTQ2+," you found nothing. No images. No articles. No links to pages on your website that announce how committed you are to LGBTQ2+ inclusion.

And therein lies the problem: ambiguity. LGBTQ2+ people regularly look for media and symbols to tell us that a space is safe, that we will be welcomed and feel included. If we don't find anything, we can only guess, which does not leave people feeling safe and secure.

There are literally hundreds of thousands of employers in this boat. That isn't to say they're *not* LGBTQ2+ inclusive, but the lack of information leaves people filling in the blanks. The key to success in attracting LGBTQ2+ people to your organization is how inclusive your brand is, and the only way people can find that out is by experiencing it themselves or looking it up online.

If you don't have anything out there yet, start with a page on your website, talking about the work you've done that's focused on LGBTQ2+ inclusion. Do you have an LGBTQ2+ Employee Resource Group? Do you sponsor LGBTQ2+

organizations or events? Are any out LGBTQ2+ leaders willing to put their profile on your website? A statement is okay,
but people want to see action. Where is the evidence that you
care, beyond the words that some poor person on your communication team stole from some other organization? Actions
speak louder than words.

Fighting a Bad Public Narrative

You have complete control over your website. If you're fighting
a bad public narrative about how you fired a person because
they were LGBTQ2+, or you're a university that had a ten-
ured professor who made international headlines because
he refused to use students' gender pronouns, then you need
to work really hard to counter that message. You have to do
everything I mention in chapter 5 about creating safe space
(reread it as many times as you need to). Then, when you've
done all that, you can start talking publicly about the work
you've done and start the healing process.

From there, you can sponsor LGBTQ2+ events and get
yourself out there into the community. Eventually your brand
will start to show up on the "nice list" instead of perpetually
being on the "naughty list."

Let's look at another example that shows just how
important this work is by focusing on the sordid tale of one
organization: Target. In 2010, Target's then CEO Gregg
Steinhafel made a big boo-boo that caused a massive ripple
effect and found the organization persona non grata with the
LGBTQ2+ communities for many years.

Up until that point, Target had a stellar reputation in the LGBTQ2+ communities. They'd supported LGBTQ2+ organizations, had an LGBTQ2+ Employee Resource Group, extended benefits to same-sex couples (before it was legally required), did LGBTQ2+ inclusive training, and regularly received a perfect score on the HRC's Corporate Equality Index.

Then Steinhafel donated $150,000 to Minnesota Forward, which purported to function as a champion of the Minnesota economy but which also funded the gubernatorial run of Representative Tom Emmer, who was opposed to marriage equality and was reported to be linked to groups that supported killing LGBTQ2+ people.[5] Worse, Steinhafel defended his donation, sending a companywide email stating: "We rarely endorse all advocated positions of the organizations or candidates we support, and we do not have a political or social agenda ... As you know, Target has a history of supporting organizations and candidates, on both sides of the aisle, who seek to advance policies aligned with our business objectives, such as job creation and economic growth ... Let me be very clear, Target's support of the GLBT community is unwavering, and inclusiveness remains a core value of our company."[6]

Nice words—but no action. And frankly, he was talking out of both sides of his mouth. After a significant public outcry, Steinhafel apologized, but Target continued to donate to anti-LGBTQ2+ politicians. According to the October 2010 filings from the Federal Elections Commission, even after the apology, Target donated another $31,200 to anti-LGBTQ2+

politicians or Political Action Committees that supported anti-LGBTQ2+ causes and candidates.[7]

The result was a massive backlash from LGBTQ2+ people and their allies. Platinum-selling singer Lady Gaga—who identifies as bisexual and has long been seen as an icon within the LGBTQ2+ communities (truthfully, for the longest time, I thought she was a really fabulous drag queen)—was working on an exclusive deal with Target, *if* they were willing to change their policies and work to make amends for their wrongdoings. The deal eventually fell apart when the two parties couldn't agree on details.[8] That deal could have been worth tens (if not hundreds) of millions of dollars for Target.

Slowly but surely, Target got back into the good graces of the LGBTQ2+ communities. It took years, but they migrated from their "we remain neutral" position when it comes to politics (a position that wasn't neutral at all, but let's keep going) to taking a stand. In 2014 they signed on as a friend of the court brief in two marriage-equality cases that eventually went to the Supreme Court, which brought us equal marriage in the United States.

The moral of the story is simple: your brand is the most important thing you possess. Don't mess with it. In the age of social media and online activism, you can't remain neutral. You have to take a stand. You don't get to play both sides of the argument. Either you're in favor of LGBTQ2+ inclusion or you're not. You can't have it both ways.

Lady Gaga is watching, and so are her more than 50 million Instagram followers.

Ready Your Recruiters

Once you're sure your brand is LGBTQ2+ friendly, you need to turn your attention to the ambassadors of your brand: your recruiters. Call them what you will—talent attraction managers, headhunters, volunteer coordinators, whatever—these people are often the first point of contact with your organization. People must have a good experience with the recruiter, or you risk losing out on superb talent.

Ask yourself: Are your recruiters prepared? And before you say, "Of course they're prepared; we're in the 2020s," it's not safe to assume that a person isn't homophobic, transphobic, or biphobic just based on the calendar year. There is an old saying about when you assume. It's annoying, and my father has been saying it for fifty years, so I'm not going to say it, but you know... ass and stuff.

There is no way to know if a person is homophobic, transphobic, or biphobic. There's also no real way to know if someone is LGBTQ2+ competent enough to hold their own while having a conversation with a person that they know, or that they suspect, is LGBTQ2+ identified.

As such, you have to assume that everyone needs education. Do your recruiters know the history of the LGBTQ2+ communities? Do they understand what they can and cannot legally ask? Do they know how to respond when a person comes out during the interview? How would they react? How would they react when they see on someone's résumé that they are/were part of an LGBTQ2+ group?

These are all vital questions. If recruiters aren't completely comfortable with the subject matter, they can really stick their foot in it. There are so many potential ways they can mess up:

- "I see you were a member of the LGBTQ2+ student group at your school. I've been dying to ask someone this. Can you please explain Trans* to me? It's so confusing."

- "OMG, you're gay? I love *RuPaul's Drag Race*. I'm a super-fan. Didn't you love it when Sasha had those rose petals hidden under her wig?"

- "You're what? Pansexual? What's that? There are so many preferences that I just can't keep up."

- "I never would've guessed that you were a man. You look so feminine. Have you had surgery?"

I could go on with the examples of how to find yourself in a lawsuit, but really, I think you get the point. People have the best of intentions when they say things like the examples above, but in doing so, they leave a terrible impression on the candidate. Although I may also be obsessed with RuPaul's drag dynasty (#DragRaceIsMyAddiction), an interview is not the right place to have a fan club meeting.

Recruiters need to be prepared. They need to be educated on LGBTQ2+ inclusion to ensure they don't make a mistake. That education should include things like:

- Proper terminology

- The difference between sexual orientation, gender identity and expression, and attraction

- Legal frameworks—what they can and can't ask

- How to practice active listening

The last and arguably most important thing they need to understand is how to sell a candidate that doesn't fit the mold. While a lot of LGBTQ2+ people have passing privilege, many don't. An example might be a non-binary person who has a beard but presents in "women's clothing" (think Jonathan Van Ness from Netflix's *Queer Eye*). How is your recruiter going to sell that candidate to the hiring manager? How are they going to present them? What are they going to say to prepare them?

Candidates who don't fit into the box are often hard to sell, even when they have all the skills and experience that you're looking for in a candidate. We all have biases, and they can kick in when we least expect. In an interview I conducted some time ago, the candidate was wearing an awkward-looking wig. My bias is always toward natural hair (or lack of hair). You see, I have some experience with wearing wigs (if you really want to know, you can likely dig up pictures on Facebook) and know how uncomfortable they can be. The entire interview I kept thinking about her wig, and I wasn't listening to what she had to say. Yes, I do realize what a vapid dick I sound like by having shared that story, but the point remains the same. The candidate didn't have a chance because my bias got in the way.

When a recruiter presents a person who might not fit into the hiring manager's preconceived notion of a "good candidate," the recruiter should prepare the hiring manager in advance. This will help the candidate and the hiring manager by ensuring there isn't an awkward moment, and the hiring manager can focus on what the candidate has to say, as opposed to how they look.

Happy Hiring Managers

The story for hiring managers (also referred to as people managers) is the same: Are they prepared? However, there's an added layer with hiring managers.

Recruiters have a pretty sweet gig: they find the candidate, get the candidate in place, and then bugger off while the hiring manager deals with the situation the recruiter leaves behind. Why does that sound like my first marriage?

The hiring manager has to address the ramifications of hiring an LGBTQ2+ person (or any person who doesn't "fit," truth be told, but that's another book). What if you did hire Jonathan Van Ness to be part of your finance team (assuming JVN actually had the skills to do the job, which I will comment on shortly)? How would people react?

That's the part the hiring manager plays. They must make sure that the culture of the work environment is LGBTQ2+ inclusive—not in the entire organization but at least in the little fiefdom that they control.

And so we come back to the idea I opened the chapter with—do the work to make sure your organization is inclusive. The hiring manager's responsibility, in conjunction with their diversity and inclusion team, is to ensure that there aren't issues of homophobia, transphobia, and biphobia in the workplace. Are your team members educated on LGBTQ2+ inclusion? Do they understand the difference between sexual orientation and gender? And so on.

If you don't do the prework, you risk hiring an LGBTQ2+ person into the organization who will then turn around and leave, file a human rights complaint, and/or sue. These are bad outcomes. You don't want these things to happen. So, make sure your recruiters and hiring managers are prepared.

The Skills

I hate that I have to include this, but I know there's someone reading this who now thinks I'm suggesting you hire a person *because* they're LGBTQ2+, regardless of whether or not they have the skills to do the job.

No, I am not suggesting that. Not even close. I will never suggest that. I will never tell you that you should hire a person because of their sexuality or gender, let alone any other personal characteristic. That's not only insulting to the person, but also a bad business decision because you're setting them up for failure. If a person doesn't have the skills to do the job, regardless of who they are or how they identify, you can't hire them. I don't care if they're a leprechaun or a unicorn; skill always takes precedence. The only exception to this rule is *if* a personal characteristic is a bona fide occupational requirement—like, if you're a bus driver, you have to be able to see.

Should you hire Jonathan Van Ness to work on your finance team? Maybe. Maybe not. I don't know JVN personally, but (and I acknowledge that this is solely based on stereotypes) I don't get a sense that he would be a numbers guy. He's incredibly talented and creative—but I can't see him in an advanced trigonometry class. It doesn't matter who the person is or how they identify; they must have the skills to do the job.

The thing that really gets me about this conversation is that I only ever hear this question raised when we're talking about underrepresented groups—women, people of color, LGBTQ2+ people, and so on. Never have I ever heard anyone say that they would have to lower their standards to hire straight white able-bodied men, or what I call SWAMs.

Why is it that when we talk about underrepresented groups, we suddenly need to consider our standards, but when it comes to SWAMs, we can find more than enough qualified candidates for the job? Either you're not getting enough candidates from said underrepresented groups applying because you're not known as an inclusive employer, or there is unconscious bias at play and you're making decisions not based on skill and ability but on your preconceived notion of what the "right" candidate looks like. It's one or the other. I'll leave you to ponder which.

Key Takeaways

- You must ensure your organization is LGBTQ2+ inclusive before you focus on talent attraction.

- Your brand is a 24-7 calling card that sends a strong message about how LGBTQ2+ inclusive your organization might be.

- Recruiters and hiring managers need to be educated so they don't mess up the interview process.

Enjoying the book?
Why not leave a review with
your favorite book seller?

★ ★ ★ ★ ★

If you're not enjoying it…
why are you still reading it?
Nothing left to watch on Netflix?

8

RETAINING LGBTQ2+ PEOPLE

If you help elect more gay people, that gives a **green light to all who feel disenfranchised**, a green light to move forward.

HARVEY MILK, civil rights activist and
the first openly LGBTQ2+ person
elected to public office in the United States

Now we're going to focus on retaining LGBTQ2+ talent. This is all about the inclusion side of diversity and inclusion. You've got the diversity; now you need to make sure all your people feel included.

First things first: Did you read chapter 5, "The Importance of Safe Space"? You're going to want to read that chapter. Maybe read it twice. Take notes, even. Use sticky tabs to highlight your favorite parts. It's an instruction manual on what you need to do to retain your LGBTQ2+ peeps. I feel like I may have mentioned that before. Perhaps it's important. It will probably be on the test.

You must ensure that yours is a safe space. If it's not, best of luck retaining people. Anecdotally, many LGBTQ2+ people will not tolerate homophobia, transphobia, or biphobia in their organization, particularly if they're open about their sexuality or gender identity. And if they report it to the powers that be and it's not addressed, they will happily address the situation themselves—by quitting, filing a human rights complaint, and/or suing. Not to mention sharing with all their friends and family what a homophobic/biphobic/transphobic organization you have.

In the chapter on safe space, I cover several topics that will help in your retention efforts, but there are a few other aspects that you may want to consider, and a few things that I'm going to expand on.

Education

I covered education previously, but it's so important that it's worth repeating. One of the biggest gaps I have seen (and one of those infamous "quick wins") is education. There is not only a woeful lack of education about LGBTQ2+ inclusion, but also a real problem with (1) how the education is being *executed* and (2) how the education is *perceived*.

Don't Do "One and Done"

At the top of the list of issues is the fact that the approach to educating on D&I is traditionally "one and done." You put everyone through a voluntary program and you're good, right? This is what I like to refer to as "wrong."

The first mistake is that your employee population isn't static. The average employee turnover rate is about 18 percent, but that can be a lot higher in some industries (like food service or retail). One food service employer I worked with, who shall remain nameless, had a turnover rate of nearly 75 percent for frontline workers. By the time you've trained everyone, you need to start back at the beginning to capture new people. And that cycle continues endlessly. Education should be part of onboarding. From the day a person starts, there should be mandatory D&I education (obviously, with specific LGBTQ2+ content) driven by a D&I learning map that takes each person through a learning journey.

The second mistake in the "one and done" approach is the idea that one program covers it all. If #BlackLivesMatter has shown us anything, it's that we have a lot of work to do to educate people on anti-Black and anti-Indigenous systemic racism. And that's just *one* topic. The conversation on LGBTQ2+ inclusion is constantly evolving, and your education program should be too.

Start with good ol' fashioned diversity and inclusion fundamentals (what D&I means and why it is important in your organization) and build from there to more complex topics like unconscious bias and cultural competence. If you don't know what these are, or if you think I'm speaking in tongues, you probably didn't read *Birds of All Feathers* 😊. These courses are the foundational building blocks of any D&I learning program, before you get into specific demographic groups. From there you can go on to LGBTQ2+ education (and this should be a series, not a single course) and so on. There are a lot of identities under the pan-diversity umbrella, and they all have different considerations. Think of it like putting all your employees through a certificate program in LGBTQ2+ inclusion and keep layering on topics as you go.

Voluntary?!

This one is so wrong it gets its own heading: Voluntary. Even "strongly encouraged" is a euphemism for "we'd really like you to... if you have the time... but if not, don't worry about it... because we don't have the nerve to make it mandatory." Many times, I have delivered training that's voluntary and found myself in a room full of smiling faces nodding at every word I say. Although I love my fans, the problem is you don't need to preach to the choir; you need to preach to the back row.

In *Birds of All Feathers*, I present a model I learned long ago called the Five Fs Continuum, which identifies five different groups that you may be dealing with in your organization.[1] The model looks like this:

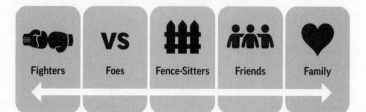

In the horrifying and unbelievable case that you haven't read my previous book, let me explain. Each one of these five groups suggests where a person might fall on the continuum based on their belief system, and in turn, how you would approach educating that group accordingly. Fighters are committed to fighting change (in this case, LGBTQ2+ inclusion) and will actively oppose it. Foes are against the change, but they're a more passive opposition. Fence-sitters are as they sound—neutral. They will not help the change, but they're also not against it. Friends are passive supporters who see the change as important but not critical. Family is committed to making the change work—they are your active supporters.[2]

When delivering "voluntary" training, you end up with an audience composed of "family," "friends," and the occasional "fence-sitter." But what you need is an audience of "fence-sitters," "foes," and "fighters." They're the ones you need to educate.

LGBTQ2+ education programs should not be "voluntary" or "strongly encouraged." Make them mandatory for all. If you really want to effect change in your organization, you have to make sure you take everyone on the journey, even if they come along kicking and screaming.

Get Everyone in the Tent

Sadly, it's not always easy to know who is homophobic, transphobic, or biphobic in your organization. It would be super helpful if they wore a badge or a hat or something. Like a red hat with writing on it. What would it say, I wonder?

That being the case, you must educate everyone. Every single person (employee, volunteer, faculty member, and so on), from the top of the house to the bottom, needs to go through the same education program. There's no way to tell who needs the education and who doesn't, so no one gets a pass.

And although I'm not delusional (enough) to believe that forcing people into LGBTQ2+ training is going to fix their homophobic, transphobic, or biphobic behavior, I like to think of education as a marathon, not a sprint. You have to take the learner on a journey of discovery, not just about other people, but about themselves. That happens over time.

Education Doesn't Have to Be Long

When leaders hear "education," they usually think, *I'm going to have to pay people to take time off work to attend this.* Yes and no.

You can keep your education short and concise. Blended learning is a great way to educate people. Start with a series of short eLearning courses, and from there, introduce short instructor-led training sessions (which can easily be done virtually... #thanksCOVID) for some or all of your people, and continue to build on their knowledge. eLearning is great for covering the fundamentals of a topic—think of it like an information push—but it doesn't allow for that engaged conversation where the real learning happens. The advantage of instructor-led training is that it allows for a much higher level of interactivity and discussion. Instructor-led training can be developed in-house, or you can bring in an external consultant to do it for you.

That said, yes, you should be paying your people to learn something that *you* want them to learn. Do you pay them to take safety and/or compliance training? Then you should pay them to take LGBTQ2+ training.

Learning Is Everywhere

Structured learning is one thing, but unstructured learning is equally as valuable. There are so many ways we learn: reading a book (like mine... just sayin'), watching a television show or movie, listening to a podcast, or having a conversation. They're all ways to expand your understanding of other people's experiences.

From an organizational perspective, how about a book club where you read, let's say, this book, and have team or group discussions about the various sections? Maybe I've even been smart enough to prepare companion guides with learning plans that are available at the end of this book and at michaelbach.com.

So many options, most involving my books. Totally coincidental.

Focus on Leaders

Leaders take center stage. They're so critical to the success of something like LGBTQ2+ inclusion. If the leaders are not bought in, it sends a signal that it's not really a priority for the organization, and as such, people fall back into their old patterns.

Make sure you put your leaders through their paces around LGBTQ2+ education. In fact, if you're introducing an LGBTQ2+ inclusive education program, wouldn't they be a great pilot audience?

Measure, Measure, Measure

I'm forever speaking about measurement—because it's important. It tells you so much. How do you know if you have been successful if you don't measure?

Just as employers monitor the application, promotion, and turnover rates of women, people of color, veterans (primarily in the United States), people with disabilities, and Indigenous peoples (among other groups), adding sexual orientation and gender identity to the list of monitored groups really goes a long way in showing how important you see LGBTQ2+ inclusion. Aside from measuring your representation of LGBTQ2+ people and their feelings of inclusion and engagement, other key indicators, such as rates of application, promotion, and voluntary and involuntary turnover, just to name a few, are important to measure too.

If you're monitoring the demographic representation of your applicant pool, you should be allowing candidates to identify by their sexual orientation and gender identity. This will help you to understand if you're successful in your talent attraction efforts with people from the LGBTQ2+ communities.

If you have a high-potential (hi-po) list and you're tracking demographics of those candidates (which you should be), make sure you include their sexual orientation and gender identity. This helps you understand if you're promoting people at the same/similar rate. If you don't have any people who identify as LGBTQ2+ on your hi-po list, it raises the question, *Why not?*

Measuring voluntary and involuntary turnover through a demographic lens acts as an early warning sign when there is an issue with a particular demographic group. If you're tracking this on an ongoing basis, you can see when LGBTQ2+ people are leaving the organization at higher rates, and then deal with it.

A warning about measurement: it's all about *self*-identification. You see how I put the emphasis on self? That means it's important.

Measuring demographic information as part of application, promotion, and voluntary and involuntary turnover is complicated. The process is about trust—that individuals trust you, so they answer the questions honestly; they trust that their answers aren't going to negatively impact their prospects of either getting, or keeping, a role with you. That's not simple. Consider that there are still countries that seek to identify LGBTQ2+ people to "reform" them or to eradicate them. That's not history. That's current. Both the United States and Canada have a patchy record of this type of behavior. Even today, as of the writing of this book, more than thirty states have bills either passed or in process that prohibit Trans* athletes from playing on teams or in leagues based on their gender identity. A bill in North Carolina goes so far as to say, "Sex shall be recognized based solely on a person's reproductive biology and genetics at birth." [3] That's not something that happened thirty years ago, in some far-off country you've never heard of. It's happening today, in your country.

Some LGBTQ2+ people may be very uncomfortable ticking the box of self-identification. You have to do a lot of work to ensure that you create a safe space for people to share that information, and then never break that trust.

Engagement

Adjacent to the conversation around measurement is the equally important conversation on engagement. It's so important that I've given it its own section. How do you know if your LGBTQ2+ people are engaged?

The concept of employee engagement is reported to have come about in 1990, stemming from an article on academic management theory called "Psychological Conditions of Personal Engagement and Disengagement at Work" by William A. Kahn.[4] Kahn was building on some research into human motivation, with the goal of understanding how employers could reduce their voluntary turnover rates. He defined engagement as an employee's ability to bring their "full self" to work, and he identified three psychological conditions that enable that: meaningfulness, safety, and availability. Any of this sounding familiar?

The point of measuring employee engagement is to understand how productive employees will be. Remember my formula from before?

High Engagement = High Productivity = High Profitability

The point many miss when measuring employee engagement is to cut their data by demographics. I recall that at one company I was working with, the person responsible for employee engagement said quite proudly to me, "We have a very high engagement score: over 80 percent." My immediate response was "That's great. Have you cut your data by demographics?"

I spent an hour trying to explain why that was important, but this person was just too stuck in the idea that identity didn't impact engagement. Amazing how wrong they were. When they finally did slice and dice their engagement data by demographics, they found that straight white able-bodied men were very engaged. Other groups ... not so much. Allow me to paint you a picture.

Let's say a question on your engagement survey reads, "I feel valued at work," and (as is the standard in these types of surveys) you have five or six responses from the Likert scale, ranging from Strongly Agree to Strongly Disagree. And let's say that 80 percent of respondents select "strongly agree" or "agree." You might think that positive sentiment is amazing. Right?

Let's segment the data by the binary sex of male and female. And let's assume for this hypothesis that there is an equal split between males and females in the organization. Now, what if males responded at 95 percent and females were responding at 65 percent? Still excited about your results? Or are you freaked out (as you should be) because that means that half your population is really feeling valued (males at 95 percent), and half your population is not feeling valued (females at 65 percent)?

It is imperative that you're looking at your employee engagement scores through demographic lenses to understand if there's an issue with a particular group. It doesn't tell you why there's an issue, just that there is one. As I always say, it doesn't tell you why there's a fire; it just tells you where to point the hose.

Because you can't assume that all people from a group share the same sentiment, looking at the data through an intersectional lens is also important. For this, I need a table.

I FEEL VALUED AT WORK	POSITIVE SENTIMENT
Overall	80%
Straight/cisgender	95%
LGBTQ2+	65%
LGBTQ2+ males	80%
LGBTQ2+ females	50%

If you look at the table above, what you see is the overall positive sentiment of 80 percent, which is great. Then you see that the straight cisgender population comes in at 95 percent, with LGBTQ2+ respondents, coming in at 65 percent. Danger, Will Robinson! for the LGBTQ2+ folks. But if we segment that data even further and look at LGBTQ2+ people who identify as male and those who identify as females, we see an even more concerning trend that LGBTQ2+ identified females are at 50 percent engagement, compared with LGBTQ2+ identified males at 80 percent.

All this is to say that you need to cut your employee engagement data by demographics, ensuring you use an intersectional approach to understand if one or more demographic groups feel less or more engaged, and then you need to figure out why that's the case.

Celebrations

As I mentioned in the chapter "The Importance of Safe Space," celebrations are an important part of creating safe space, but they're also an important part of retaining LGBTQ2+ people.

As an LGBTQ2+ person, particularly if I'm not open about my identity, the thing that I am looking for is that visible sign that I'm going to be safe. Many LGBTQ2+ people have faced rejection in their lives—from friends, family, and even random strangers. We don't and won't risk coming out if we're not nearly 100 percent certain that the space is one where we will be welcomed.

You can't insist that people come out, but as an organization, your role is to create an environment where people can, should they choose, come out and trust that they will be safe and welcomed.

Celebrations are an important part of signaling that. In celebrating LGBTQ2+ Pride Month, or National Coming Out Day, or International Transgender Day of Visibility (just to name a few of the many you could choose from), you communicate that you respect the diversity of your employees. Regardless of whether or not a person is out, you send a message that they *can* be out. You are saying that you respect people's identities—without *telling* them you respect their identities. Words are great. But as John Pym, the English parliamentarian, said in 1628, "A word spoken in season is like an Apple of Gold set in Pictures of Silver, and actions are more precious than words."[5]

Zero-ish Tolerance

Equally important to providing safe space is having a zero-tolerance policy that is actually seen in practice. I talked about this in the chapter on safe space, but I'm going to contradict myself a tiny bit. Because it's my book and I want to.

What is zero tolerance? "Zero tolerance is a way to eliminate undesirable behavior among employees and provide an automatic punishment for violating company rules. These policies keep those in managerial roles from bending the rules or using their own discretion."[6]

There are various instances when a zero-tolerance policy is automatic, and it should be. You embezzle millions from your company pension plan? Yup, you're out. You sexually assault someone? Buh-bye. You get super drunk at a company holiday party, strip down naked, and run around wrapped in a curtain, doing your best Carol Channing impersonation, rattling on about eating corn? Please seek professional help.

But there are gray areas to take into consideration. When the behavior is obvious, making a clear-cut decision to fire the offender is simple. But how often is the behavior obvious compared to the subtlety of microinequities and microaggressions? Uh oh. New words. Need to define those.

The term "microinequity" was defined in 1973 by Mary Rowe, a professor at MIT, as "small events that may be ephemeral and hard to prove; that may be covert, often unintentional, and frequently unrecognized by the perpetrator; that occur wherever people are perceived to be different; and that can cause serious harm, especially in the aggregate."[7] Think of them as tiny little words and actions. They're hard to prove. But the impact of them is unquestionable, like death by a thousand paper cuts.

Imagine that someone is giving a presentation while several people tap away on their smartphones. The presenter has no idea what they're doing on their phones—they could be taking notes or playing Candy Crush—but the impact on the presenter is just the same. They feel like the people aren't interested in and don't care about what they have to say. Or, perhaps, in a meeting Joe says something and Tasha rolls her eyes. Or what if you are having a conversation with someone and they look at their watch? What message are you receiving from that person's actions? Or what if you are orienting a new person to your organization and you introduce your colleague Amir by speaking about him with glowing accolades, and standing beside him is Dev, whom you introduce by name alone. Amir feels great. Dev feels terrible.

First introduced by Harvard University psychologist Chester Pierce in the 1970s, a microaggression is "a subtle behavior—verbal or non-verbal, conscious or unconscious—directed at a member of a marginalized group that has a derogatory, harmful effect."[8] Microaggressions are like microinequities on steroids.

An example of a microaggression is failing to learn how to properly pronounce a student's name, or worse, continuing to mispronounce it after you've been corrected. Every time you say that student's name incorrectly, they are reminded of how little you care about them, and it's not a good feeling. Or you're a white man or woman and you reach out and touch a Black woman's hair without warning and without asking if it's okay. Every Black person reading this book is nodding in agreement. Every white person is sure I just made that up. I didn't. Ask your Black friends how many times that's happened to them.

While microinequities and microaggressions sound similar, there are distinct differences: microaggressions are innately "aggressive" in nature, and they are always directed at a person from a marginalized group, whereas a microinequity can be directed at anyone.

The truth is that we're constantly seeing microinequities and microaggressions in the workplace. Now, let's connect that back to the LGBTQ2+ communities. What if I'm in a conversation about what my husband and I did on the weekend, and the person I'm talking to says, "Which one of you is the wife?" How am I supposed to take that? There are many options: I can ignore it and change the topic of conversation; I can laugh it off or make a joke about it; or I can put myself in the position of educator and explain how that gender stereotype is offensive and suggest that they educate themselves.

And before you think that doesn't happen, it happened to me last week.

But is that grounds for zero tolerance? If it goes against my organization's code of conduct, arguably the answer is yes. However, it's really hard to prove. They were just making a joke. I should lighten up and not take it so seriously, right?

This is where we enter the gray area of zero tolerance. How do you prove the offense happened, keeping in mind that employers have legal responsibilities? In some places, you can fire people for any reason, let alone for doing something that goes against your code of conduct. But in many jurisdictions, there are labor laws that prohibit dismissal without grounds. And those grounds have to be pretty rock-solid, or you'll find yourself in court and/or paying a pretty hefty severance.

My opinion, for what it's worth, is that employers need to follow a *zero-ish* tolerance approach. For the clear-cut cases, the decision is straightforward. You break the rules, you're out, with no debate. And take note, employers: that may mean you have to fire someone who is a "rock star performer." Certain acts deserve zero tolerance, and if you don't stick by that rule just because a person brings a lot of money into your organization, you will inevitably erode trust, and your zero-tolerance policy will be looked at as the joke that it is.

But for the cases that are a little harder to prove, I believe in giving the offender the opportunity to learn from their mistakes. Not that you shouldn't do anything, but the punishment should be commensurate with the crime. If someone makes a stupid joke, they should have to take some training to understand why their joke was inappropriate. They should have to learn from their mistakes and apologize for their wrongdoings. Some people will realize the error of their ways. Others won't see the problem, and they'll repeat similar behaviors. So maybe instead of one strike, they get two. First mistake, you learn from it and improve. Make the mistake again, and you have no place in the organization.

The same applies in other environments. A college or university with a zero-ish tolerance approach would grant any student, faculty, or staff found to be making homophobic, transphobic, or biphobic comments or actions the opportunity to go through some training, or to work with a coach to understand why their behavior was inappropriate. If it doesn't change, they are no longer welcome on campus. If a religious- or faith-based organization decides that it's going to be inclusive of LGBTQ2+ members, and another member of the organization exhibits homophobic, transphobic, or biphobic behavior, then the offender should be led through some LGBTQ2+ inclusion training to ensure that they are abiding by the organization's position. Or they can pray elsewhere.

You can't tolerate inappropriate behavior, but it's important to consider it relatively and respond accordingly. Repeat offenders get the boot. No exceptions.

Rewards and Benefits

Another consideration around retention of LGBTQ2+ people relates to your rewards and benefits. Beyond base compensation, what does your rewards and benefits plan include, and are there considerations about whether your rewards and benefits meet the needs of LGBTQ2+ people? To help you get your mind around this, I am going to share a few examples of how the needs of LGBTQ2+ people may be different.

Parental Leave

Do you have a "maternity leave" policy or a "parental leave" policy? A maternity leave policy is and should be different from a parental leave policy. Maternity leave is a term that is defined in law. In most instances, maternity leave benefits are available only to the person who is away from work because they're pregnant or have given birth. It's specific and involves precise legal requirements for how long a person can be off, the financial benefit they will receive (usually captured under Employment Insurance, or UI in the States, and/or with an employer's top-up), and how long an employer is required to hold their job for them.

Parental leave is a relatively different concept. Parental leave can relate to anyone who is a parent, regardless of their role: biological parents, adoptive parents, those using surrogacy, and so on. Consider that family models have changed a tiny bit since Ward and June Cleaver were chasing after the Beaver, but have your parental leave policies kept up? Are fathers permitted to take time off, paid or not? Do you have a top-up for people who need to use medical assistance to get pregnant? Do you have a program that provides a financial reward for people who adopt? These benefits should be available to anyone, regardless of their identity and regardless of how the child comes into their family.

One important thing to consider: men *can* have babies. Wait, what? You heard me, and I'm not just talking about the three minutes of their involvement in procreation. Consider that there are people who identify as men who have had babies. One such story is that of Freddy McConnell, a Trans* man who carried his son, Jack, through pregnancy.[9]

I know some people have just crossed their eyes, so let me break it down for you. Freddy was assigned female at birth. He was born with female reproductive organs, meaning biologically he could carry a child. At twenty-five, McConnell began his transition and started taking testosterone and had top surgery (the removal of his breasts), but he didn't have bottom surgery (a hysterectomy) because he hadn't ruled out the possibility of children. At some point he decided he wanted a child, so he stopped taking testosterone and, through a sperm donor, became pregnant and had a son.

This is where we have to differentiate between sex and gender. Freddy was still physically capable of getting pregnant. And he made the choice to bring his son into the world. That act does not make him any less of a man. He's just a man who gave birth to a baby.

It's important to keep in mind the fact that maternity isn't just for "women"—it is for anyone who is able to have a child biologically. And parental leave is for anyone who becomes a parent.

Transition Guidelines

Stop me if you've heard this one. An employee walks into your office and tells you they're transitioning genders, and you start to fumble and spout off like an idiot because you don't know what that entails. Such a funny moment. I can see Melissa McCarthy really crushing that comedy gold. Except it's not too funny for the employee.

Do you have a Workplace Gender Transition Guideline? You should. It's a plan that does exactly what it sounds like—it helps the employer and the employee go through the process of transition. It includes information on things like how to tell coworkers, how to address issues of restroom access, and how to monitor signs of resentment and hostility.

My friends at the Human Rights Campaign have created a beautiful Template for Gender Transition Guidelines that you can leverage to create your own.[10] Remember, if you fail to plan, you plan to fail.

Transition Assistance

Beyond having a Workplace Gender Transition Guideline, do you have any coverage to assist the employee with transition? The process of transition is expensive, depending on what is involved. If you have both top and bottom surgery, that cost alone can be in the tens if not hundreds of thousands. Then there's the cost of medications, new clothing, changes in name and identification, and so on. In Canada, although transition is covered in all ten provinces and one territory, a great deal of costs are not covered. In the United States, private insurance coverage ranges wildly. It changes from state to state, just as much as it does from one employer to the next.

A leading practice to retain LGBTQ2+ people is to assist employees who are transitioning. This is a big benefit and can cost a significant amount, but consider that only a small percentage of the population will take advantage of it.

Regardless of the number of people who will benefit, transition assistance sends a robust signal about the inclusivity of your organization for LGBTQ2+ people.

Drug Coverage

You might be thinking this one is obvious, but you are so incorrect. Insurance coverage for medications is not created equally. So you must work with your insurance provider to understand which drugs are covered and which are not. For instance, medications to treat HIV/AIDS are ridiculously expensive and can cost as much as several thousand dollars per month. That's not to say that HIV/AIDS is a "gay disease," but a percentage of the LGBTQ2+ population live with HIV, and to keep living, they need their antiretroviral meds. Does your health plan include coverage? And what about coverage for PrEP drugs? This stands for pre-exposure prophylaxis, which has been proved as highly effective in reducing the spread of HIV to nearly zero.

If you don't know the answers, you've likely never asked. Most insurance companies will limit coverage for drugs they view as unnecessary, but for some people those drugs could be lifesaving, and offering them will send a clear message about your support of your LGBTQ2+ employees.

Celebration of Milestones

Beyond the traditional health benefits, where else are there opportunities to create more inclusion? What about milestone events? Do you celebrate key milestones in your workplace—for example, when someone has a child or gets married? Do you do that for LGBTQ2+ people as well? If not, why not?

When I got married, my boss (who, to be clear, was a straight white able-bodied man) organized a surprise celebration with all of HR (the department I worked in). I was asked to meet him in the lunchroom, and I walked into a big surprise celebration of my nuptials. It was an amazing feeling to have all my colleagues around me celebrating my relationship (particularly because I hadn't invited most of them to the wedding, which was a wee bit awkward).

And why wouldn't my employer do that? We celebrated all sort of things (I secretly think it was just any excuse to have cake, which I am so down with), so why not celebrate the marriage of one Michael to another (you know... because his name is Michael too). Acts like that normalize LGBTQ2+ identities and build engagement and trust.

The Extra Perks

You likely provide your employees with lots of perks. For example, do you award a luxury trip to your top salespeople each year? If so, what is the destination for that trip? Have you looked into the laws related to LGBTQ2+ people in that country, considering that there are seventy-one countries where being gay or lesbian is illegal? You might think taking your leadership team and their spouses on a trip to Jamaica is a fantastic idea—but consider that it excludes people who are gay or lesbian because of that country's laws around sexuality and gender. Or what if your church group is going on a mission to Antigua and Barbuda? Your LGBTQ2+ parishioners could end up serving fifteen years in prison just because of their relationship.

Straight cisgender people don't necessarily think of these kinds of issues, and you don't need to, if it's just about you. It doesn't need to cross your mind because your safety, as a straight and cisgender person, is not in jeopardy when you're swimming in the crystal blue waters of Montego Bay. But if you want to be inclusive of your LGBTQ2+ people, it's an important consideration to pick a destination that is inclusive of everyone.

Travel is just one example of many I could use, but the point is, when you're looking at all the perks you offer to your employees, are you peering through an LGBTQ2+ lens to ensure you aren't inadvertently excluding anyone?

Gender-Inclusive Restrooms

This one falls into the category of, *Do I really have to explain this to people?* but I do, so let's just get on with it. Make sure you provide gender inclusive restrooms. Enough said?

It may seem like a silly thing to consider, but if you're Trans* or gender non-conforming, it's a huge deal. If you've shown up as your true self, particularly for this first time, a big concern is where you can pee in private. Gender-inclusive restrooms also signal to LGBTQ2+ people that the space is inclusive.

The leading practice is simple: provide a private restroom that anyone can use and that is fully accessible and has a lock on the door. If that's not possible, make your restrooms unisex, with floor-to-ceiling stalls so no one can peek. Then everyone uses the same bathroom. Put cameras in to monitor activity outside the stalls. This may be controversial, but it also helps protect against violence.

And don't get cute with the sign. I don't go to the bathroom for the laughs. I've seen so many restroom signs that are hurtful, diminishing, and promote gender as a binary. If you look at the image below, you have a male figure, a female figure, and a half-and-half, meaning if you're not male or female, you must be half of each. Wrong. The best practice, in my opinion, is to use an image of a toilet. That, by and large, is universally understood and no words are required. Most people who see that symbol on a door will understand what happens in that room.

Policies and Procedures

When it comes to your policies and procedures, you might be thinking, *Do I need to have a separate LGBTQ2+ policy?* And the answer to that question is ... no. You do not need a separate policy or procedure for LGBTQ2+ people. Although now that I'm thinking about it, wouldn't it be fun if every time someone self-identified as LGBTQ2+, there was an immediate flash mob to one of ABBA's greatest hits? So fun. Moving on.

You do not need a separate policy or procedure, but you need to use overt language in your existing policies and procedures. If you have an anti-harassment and/or antidiscrimination policy, specifically and explicitly include sexual orientation, gender identity, and gender expression as prohibited grounds for discrimination, and provide examples of what homophobic, transphobic, or biphobic discrimination looks like (for example, an organization suggesting that a Trans* person use the restroom of the sex they were assigned at birth, as opposed to their gender; an insurer insisting that a man applying for insurance take an HIV test because of the indication on his application of his male partner; or a colleague accusing a bisexual person of being greedy or confused). According to a report from Great Places to Work, 74 percent of organizations have policies that prohibit discrimination based on sexual orientation, but only 51 percent of those include gender identity and gender expression.[11]

Consider the language that you use in policies, and specifically whether it is gender-neutral. When referring to individuals singularly, do you still use the pronouns "he/she" or "him/her"? Why not just say "they/them"? Gender-neutral language sends a strong message, particularly to those who do not identify with the binary of "he" and "she."

Continuing along these lines, most organizations still haven't caught up in the language as it relates to gender markers. For example, when you start a new job, you may be required to complete a form and indicate your sex, where often the only options are M and F.

As you know by now, M and F are not the only options. There's an "I" that should be in there too. On top of that, what question are you asking? Do you want to know a person's sex or a person's gender? You know by now that the M and F relate to sex, not gender.

Most people don't know the difference, but if you've gotten this far, you will (or you really haven't been paying attention). What most employers want to know is gender, but they inadvertently end up asking about sex.

If you're asking about sex, then to be inclusive you should provide the three options—F, I, and M (because I like alphabetical order). But why do you want or need to know this? In many cases it's required under law—law that hasn't been updated in a generation and has no bearing on employment—but you have no choice in the matter. You really don't need to know a person's sex. That should be and is quite irrelevant.

If what you really want to know is gender, then you need to provide options for people beyond the binary of man and woman. The best practice here is to allow people to write it in, so they can write whatever they like, based on how they identify. If that won't work, include as many options as you can—be that genderqueer, gender-fluid, gender non-conforming, or even gender fabulous. Don't fall into the trap of "man," "woman," and "other." That reinforces the idea that there is still a binary, and that approach isn't inclusive.

Recently, I had the pleasure of working with a health care organization that was willing to go through the painful process of reviewing all their documentation and processes, to consider where they *were* asking patients about their sex and/or gender, and where they *should* be asking. The organization operates in multiple jurisdictions across Canada, and it provides both health insurance and health care services. The process of moving away from the binary of M and F was a significant one and involved multiple stakeholders and months of work.

In the end, the organization scoured every point of contact with a patient or client and asked one question: What are we asking (sex or gender), and do we really need this information? The result was the adjustment of multiple forms and intake documents to ensure that the language they were using was reflective of current standards around gender, and that where they didn't need to ask the question, they stopped asking.

Communications

Communications is a critical function of an organization, in that it relays information, both internally and externally, for any reason. And that means that your communications materials have the power to be inclusive—or exclusive.

Take the images you use. As advertising executive Fred R. Barnard purportedly said in 1921, "A picture is worth a thousand words." If that's true, ten thousand words is worth a hundred pictures. I have no idea where I'm going with this analogy, but I was curious who came up with that phrase. And actually, what he said was, "One look is worth a thousand words," and then he updated it to say, "Chinese proverb: one picture is worth ten thousand words." This was all to promote his ad agency, and it was all fabricated and had nothing to do with a Chinese proverb.[12] I was today years old when I learned that.

If you use images of people in your communications, do you ensure that they present the broadest range of diversity, including LGBTQ2+ people? We are seeing this more and more in the public sphere with companies putting their LGBTQ2+ inclusion front and center. Campbell's Soup, Kodak, Coca-Cola, Ray-Ban, Allstate, Absolut Vodka, Bud Light, and Lush (to name but a few) have all done advertising campaigns that explicitly include LGBTQ2+ people.[13]

What you say externally is an important consideration, but so is what you say internally. Do you communicate with your people using inclusive language? Is it gender-neutral? Do you use images that are inclusive of LGBTQ2+ people? Do you avoid gender stereotypes, like women in skirts and men in suits? What you say is just as important as how you say it, and it can go a long way to convey inclusivity.

Leadership Development

I specifically left leadership development until last in this chapter because this is a tough one for people to get their heads around: the idea that LGBTQ2+ people should have specific leadership development programs. Leadership development is applicable to workplaces, of course, but also to volunteer and faith-based organizations, colleges and universities, and any place where people direct others in some way. It is not safe to assume that all people have leadership skills. They need to be taught, and you must apply an LGBTQ2+ lens to those lessons.

Stanford University has a specific LGBTQ Executive Leadership Program designed to advance the careers of LGBTQ2+ individuals. From their website: "This highly-specialized, one-week program gives you the strategic insights, personal leadership skills, design thinking innovation, and powerful network to accelerate your career."[14] Thomas Wurster, one of the creators of the program, has said that the benefit of the program is "that it takes topics that are important to all leaders—presence, communication, power, authority—but integrates them with identity."[15]

Every LGBTQ2+ person has experienced walking into a room full of strangers and having to assess whether it is okay for them to be themselves. Can they speak about their same-sex spouse? Can they be out as LGBTQ2+? Are they going to be assumed to be straight and/or cisgender by default and have to take on the role of the educator? This takes a lot of effort, and often the answers are unclear until we take a risk and are open about our identity.

Although it would be nice if every LGBTQ2+ person could go to Stanford, that prospect is unlikely. As such, your leadership development program must be safe for people to be their authentic selves without fear of repercussion. Creating that is a not a simple process. It's everything that I've spoken about in this chapter and then some. It's a journey that your organization must go on to ensure your culture is inclusive for LGBTQ2+ people; that you are able to address issues of homophobia, transphobia, and biphobia as they present; and that your people are educated on the issues and understand their role in creating an inclusive culture for all.

Key Takeaways

- Every single person in your organization plays a role in ensuring it is inclusive for LGBTQ2+ people.

- Enforcing a zero-tolerance policy is important, as is understanding that such policies must allow gray areas. Giving people the opportunity to learn is good for the employer and the employee.

- How you communicate is just as important as what you communicate, and those messages can ensure that LGBTQ2+ people see themselves within your organization.

9

YOU MEASURE WHAT YOU TREASURE

The Lord is my

Shepherd and

He knows **I'm gay.**

TROY D. PERRY, founder of the
Metropolitan Community Church,
a Protestant denomination that
specializes in welcoming LGBTQ2+ people

am regularly asked about measurement. It's sort of my jam. Or jelly. Whatever. The point is that because of my work history (I worked in the IT space for a big chunk of my career), I have a lot of experience with how to measure the success—or the "return on investment"—of diversity and inclusion. But that's not what this chapter is about. If you want to know about how to measure your diversity and inclusion progress, check out chapter 8 of *Birds of All Feathers*, "Measurement for Success."

The chapter you are about to read is about how to measure the representation of your LGBTQ2+ employees, which is often done through a broader survey on diversity and inclusion.

The first question I always get asked about this topic is, "*Can* we ask about people's sexual orientation and gender identity?" The answer is yes, you can. But there's a catch. Before you can ask, you must:

- Give the respondent the ability to opt out. You can still make answering mandatory, but there must be a "prefer not to answer" option for every question.

- Provide a crystal-clear privacy statement that explains why you're asking, who will have access to the data, and what you're going to use it for.

- Ensure the answers will not affect employment—positively or negatively.

These three rules are specifically based on Canadian legislation. In the United States, the rules around this are less strict, but I would encourage all employers to follow the Canadian way in order to be sure that you don't end up with some unintended consequences. You don't want to find yourself on the wrong end of a lawsuit because of how you asked questions or what you did with the information. That's not to say you shouldn't ask, just that you need to be careful about the process.

Both Canada and the United States (and many other countries) have laws requiring some employers to collect personal demographic information from their employees, but none (to my/Google's knowledge) *require* employers to ask about sexual orientation and/or gender identity. In fact, if you ask the governing bodies that have oversight for said laws (Employment and Social Development Canada and the Equal Employment Opportunity Commission in the United States), they'll likely tell you *not* to ask about sexual orientation and gender identity—but that's because these are not covered by the laws in either country. Bureaucrats tend to be sticklers for what the books say.

Another question I get asked is, "Why does it matter to measure sexual orientation and gender identity?" Mostly this question comes from straight cisgender people. But remember—straight and cis until proved otherwise. As an LGBTQ2+ person, I want to know that you're thinking about me when you're devising your D&I survey. I want to know that I matter to you. Whenever I answer personal questions and the only options under the question of gender are "man" and "woman," I'm reminded of how LGBTQ2+ people are often forgotten, ignored, or just not part of the consideration. Asking shows you care. And that matters.

Plus, if you don't ask, you don't know. If you don't know how many LGBTQ2+ people you have, how do you know if you should be focused on an LGBTQ2+ volunteer recruitment strategy? If you don't allow people to identify by their sexual orientation and gender identity as part of your inclusion or engagement survey, how do you know if your workplace or school or community is LGBTQ2+ inclusive?

You have to ask to find out. And once you know, you have to do something with the data. So, here are a few considerations specifically related to asking your people about their sexual orientation and gender identity.

Know Why You're Asking

Before you ask, you need to know why you're asking. You can't ask just because you want to. I can't just walk into someone's house and start drinking their wine just because I feel like it... or so I've been told by several police officers in a variety of jurisdictions.

If you don't know why you're asking, you are just trying to satisfy morbid curiosity, and that is not a good enough reason for people to share private personal information with you. More importantly, before you can convince your organization's leadership team, and your employee population, that you need to collect this information, you need to have a rock-solid statement of purpose. There are lots of reasons why you could be asking:

- To ensure your employee population is reflective of available talent

- To understand if your LGBTQ2+ employees are feeling included

- To show that you are an LGBTQ2+ inclusive organization

Okay, that's not "a lot of reasons" as much as it is three. I could only come up with those three, but those three are good enough reasons to ask. The bottom line is that you need to know who your people are and how they feel in order to know if you have a problem that needs to be addressed. Otherwise you're just a hammer looking for a nail. Or is it a nail looking for a hammer?

My point is that once you decide the reasons you are asking, articulate them clearly so that you can convince people that asking is a good idea—and more importantly, that answering is worthwhile.

Do Something with the Data

Once you have the data, you have to do something with it. To ask the questions and then leave people hanging is cruel. Like reading my text message and then not responding. Or worse, you starting to type so I see the   icon on my screen, but you never finish. That is *maddening*! Did you get distracted? Did your mom call you for dinner? Did armed terrorists break into your house, and they're now holding you hostage until you give up the location of the super-secret base of operations? Why can't you finish writing what you were going to say?!

I digress... and am clearly working through something. Once you have the data, you have to do something with it. Here are a few ideas about what to do with the data.

Analyze it. What does the data tell you? What does your representation look like? Did you learn anything from the data? Are your LGBTQ2+ employees more or less engaged? Analyze it to better understand what the data is telling you.

Address the pink unicorn. If there is an issue, what's the plan to address it? Once you've identified a problem area, the onus is on you to figure out a solution. Ignoring it won't make it go away—in fact, it could get worse.

Sharing is caring. Your employees answered the questions. Wouldn't it be fun to share with them what you found out? How about some communications that share the results of your analysis, any issues that you identified, and your plan to address those issues? What a novel idea. And be forewarned:

people want to know, and if you don't share with them—or worse, you stick your head in the sand and tell them everything is rosy—they will not be amused. Be honest and share what you found out, no matter how bad it is. Forewarned is forearmed.

Avoid Othering

The worst thing you can do to people is "other" them. The term "othering" describes the act of diminishing a person's identity by referring to them as "other."[1] When you include a question about a person's gender and the options are man, woman, and other, a person who doesn't identify as either a man or a woman will be left feeling less valued by the simple omission of an identity that matches their own.

When you are collecting data, I strongly discourage you from using the option of "other" anywhere. That said, you're not going to use a complete and definitive list of sexual orientations and gender identities. Facebook allows users to identify with any of fifty-eight genders.[2] Good for Facebook, but not great for your data-collection process.

The leading practice is to include a list of more common sexual orientations and gender identities, and then an option that allows individuals to write in an answer that is not on your list. That way everyone's identity matters, regardless of how few people select any one particular identity.

How Should You Ask?

How you ask is critically important. You need to be careful about how you ask so as not to offend the intended audience. You are going to offend people—that's guaranteed—but you don't want to offend members of the LGBTQ2+ community, whom you're trying to include.

Use Two Questions

Remember how I told you that the LGBTQ2+ initialism is representative of two groups: sexually diverse and gender diverse folks? That being the case, you need to ask two questions, not one. If you don't remember that, please go back and read chapters 2 and 3 again, and again, until you retain the information.

The first question is about sexual orientation, which includes heterosexual. Again, include a list of the more "commonly" chosen identities, and then add a write-in option.

The second question is about gender, which includes cisgender men and women. You may or may not use the term "cisgender" (although using it is a great learning moment), but at the very least, don't use "woman," "man," and "other."

The thing you don't want to do (or the thing I'm telling you that you don't want to do) is ask only if someone is a member of the LGBTQ2+ community. Why? Because you may be double-dipping.

Remember my friend Jenn? She's a Trans* woman but is also queer. A person can be straight and Trans*. A person can be gay and non-binary. The two things are interrelated but not interconnected. Repeat after me: sexual orientation and gender identity are not the same thing. If you double-dip, you're missing part of the story.

Is There a List?

There are lots of lists. Some of them are good. Some of them are offensive. Just because I'm nice, I'm including a list below with the options available through CCDI Consulting's Diversity Meter service, as of this writing. This isn't a definitive list, and it changes regularly, but it has been built up over the years to include the more commonly selected options, along with the ability for people to share their own response.

Sex:
☐ Female   ☐ Intersex   ☐ Male   ☐ Prefer not to answer

Gender:
☐ Man   ☐ Queer   ☐ Trans*   ☐ Two-spirit   ☐ Woman
☐ Another identity not included above (please share here)
☐ Prefer not to answer

Sexual Orientation:
☐ Asexual   ☐ Bisexual   ☐ Gay   ☐ Heterosexual
☐ Lesbian   ☐ Pansexual   ☐ Queer   ☐ Questioning
☐ Two-spirit
☐ Another identity not included above (please share here)
☐ Prefer not to answer

It's a Learning Moment

When you ask, it's also a great opportunity to educate people on the differences between identities. The best way to do this is to include a glossary of the less commonly known identities on the screen so that you can educate your people as they're answering the questions.

For example, the term "Two-spirit" often confuses people. Having read this book, you know that it is traditionally used by Native American and Indigenous communities to identify people with qualities or who fulfill roles of both feminine and masculine genders, and it refers to sexual orientation, gender identity, or both. But not everyone in your organization is going to read this book. (Or *are* they? What a great idea. Operators are standing by to take your order.)

Differentiate between Sex and Gender

As you know by now, sex and gender aren't the same thing. So, which one matters? And which one should you ask about? Both. They both matter, but remember that you need to know *why* you are asking so you can understand *what* you are asking. Why is the information relevant to employing people, engaging with volunteers or students, or your ability to provide service or operate?

Are you asking because it is legally required? For example, the labor laws of every state in the United States and every province and territory in Canada require every new employee to fill out a form upon hire and to identify their sex (whether or not they *should* have to is another book). If that's the case, it is acceptable to ask. But then you must determine *what* you are asking. Are you required to ask about sex or gender? Be specific. And ensure you tell the person that you are asking because it is legally required, and under what law.

Are you asking because you think you need to know? If you are trying to determine what your representation of LGBTQ2+ people is so you can determine if you have a lack of LGBTQ2+ students, volunteers, or employees, then that's also okay. However, be very careful. Privacy commissioners have been clear that there must be a legally justifiable reason as to why you need personal information such as sex or gender. Seriously consider why you need the information. It's perfectly allowable to ask, but you should consider how it's going to impact employment or your ability to provide service. Why does it matter?

The general rule should be that you ask only when you absolutely must know, based on something you're trying to achieve. For example, why does it matter that I have my sex on my driver's license? How does that impact my experience as a driver, or a police officer's ability to enforce the speed limit? (I was not doing eighty in a forty, thank you. Your thingy is busted.)

Again, more often than not, what you really want to know is gender, not sex. It doesn't really matter what someone has going on under their clothes. What matters is how a person identifies. Asking about gender is asking how a person identifies, not how you identify them. It has nothing to do with their physical characteristics or what sex they were assigned at birth. It's very personal and individual.

Where Should You Ask?

It's important to consider the medium in which you are asking about a person's gender or sexual orientation. For cisgender people, the question is relatively common and of little consequence. They are simply a man or a woman. They have answered this question their entire life and have little concern about the response.

For a Trans* or non-binary person, a question about their sex or gender may be fraught with anxiety and fear. Consider that each will be at a different point on their journey of gender exploration, and as such will have differing comfort levels with their responses.

Being asked and answering this question in writing may be easier for some respondents, and it may provide a higher level of comfort, compared to being asked in person. When asking this question in person, such as when you're completing an intake process for a patient, before the person being asked responds, the person asking must first articulate why they need the information.

Further, when a person is asked in writing, it must be possible for the respondent's answer to be recorded as provided. If the respondent indicated they are non-binary, then that option should be available in the system where it is being recorded, as opposed to just marking them as "other." The ideal state is that you have a list of available genders to select from, and if the person identifies by an identity that's not on the list, the person recording it can add it in as provided. There are a few places that you might be collecting data to consider.

Your HR Information System

If you are on a "self-serve" Human Resources Information System (HRIS), where each person can update their own information, you can ask there. In an ideal world, you'll have the technology in place to ask the questions in your existing HRIS because then you will be able to analyze the data in all sorts of ways, like looking at the demographic makeup of promotions, voluntary turnover, and the like.

There are some downsides to this, specifically the ability to keep the data private and confidential, but the situation has been improving. The key is to ensure, as much as you can, that the responses are confidential, so no individual (or as few people as possible) can see how another person answers, and so that the data will never be used against a person.

A Third-Party Vendor

If you don't have an HRIS, or your HRIS won't allow you to ask the questions anonymously, then you can turn to a third party for this type of service. This is also helpful if you're not dealing with employees and are collecting information from students, volunteers, and so on. Selfishly, I will mention that CCDI Consulting's Diversity Meter service, which is an excellent qualitative and quantitative online measurement tool, is completely secure and anonymous. But there are others. They're just not as good because they're not mine.

The real added value of using a third party is the perception (whether accurate or not) that the data is somehow more private and confidential. Keep in mind that you're asking about very personal information. People will question—particularly the first time you run the survey—why you're asking and what will happen with the information. Using a third party can alleviate some of the stress and suspicion that people will have when you start asking.

An Engagement Survey

Regardless of whether you have an HRIS, an engagement survey is another great medium through which to allow people to self-identify. Any engagement survey provider worth their salt will be able to include demographic questions so you can analyze your engagement scores through a demographic lens. If they don't, they are not worth their salt. Or pepper. Or any seasoning at all.

It's in the Cloud

One of the most important considerations about collecting data is where the data is stored. With all due respect, Survey Monkey is not a good way to ask people deep, personal questions. I talk about this in *Birds of All Feathers*, and it's worth repeating.

People speak of "the cloud" as though it were an actual place. Like Lando Calrissian is running a server farm in Cloud City. He is not. Because he is not a real person. And Cloud City is not a real place.

When we say our data is "in the cloud," what we mean is that it is on the Internet. Data is stored on servers, and servers are located on good old terra firma—which means that wherever the server is physically located, your data is subject to the local laws of that country. If your data is on servers located in Canada, it is subject to Canada's Privacy Act. This is a good thing, particularly when you're asking a lot of personal questions about your people's sexual orientation and gender identity. If it's stored on a server in the United States, it's subject to laws like the Patriot Act. Although I mean no offense to the Patriot Act, the US government can demand access to that data if they feel it is a matter of national defense. I struggle to see how my sexual orientation or gender identity could be a matter of national defense (first rule of the gay mafia is don't talk about the gay mafia), but I can see how easy it would be for some unscrupulous people to get up to no good in the name of so-called national defense. If you're thinking that could never happen... allow me to tell you a couple of stories.

In 1961, the Canadian government hired Professor Frank Robert Wake of Carleton University in Ottawa, Ontario, to create a test to identify homosexuals hiding in the civil service, the Canadian military, and the Royal Canadian Mounted Police. Throughout the 1940s and 1950s, the government had been investigating suspected homosexuals (events commonly referred to as the LGBT Purge[3]), but the process they were using was too time-consuming and costly, so they hired Wake to devise a test to do the work for them.

Enter the Fruit Machine. It wasn't a machine, nor was there any fruit involved, but it was a series of psychological tests, including one used to detect how a person's pupils responded to images of naked or semi-naked men and women.

The Fruit Machine never worked. Although it was retired in the late 1960s, the RCMP collected over nine thousand files of suspected LGBTQ2+ folks. The process of trying to identify LGBTQ2+ people within Canada's civil service ruined careers and lives—and it was in place until as late as the early 1990s.

The United States also has a sad history as it relates to hunting down LGBTQ2+ people. Besides things like Don't Ask, Don't Tell (DADT) and the prohibition of Trans* people in the military, McCarthyism in the 1940s and 1950s significantly impacted LGBTQ2+ people, as they were caught up in the country's infamous Lavender Scare.

The Second Red Scare ran from the late 1940s through the 1950s (the First Red Scare occurred just after World War I) as panic over perceived Communist infiltration swept through the nation. In 1947, President Truman signed Executive Order 9835 to screen federal employees for affiliation with organizations deemed "totalitarian, fascist, communist, or subversive," or advocating "to alter the form of Government of the United States by unconstitutional means."[4] While giving a speech in 1950, Senator Joseph McCarthy presented a list of people working in the State Department who were alleged members of the Communist Party. This attracted a lot of press and eventually led to the creation of the House

Un-American Activities Committee. The primary targets of suspicion were government employees, labor union activities, academics, and those in the entertainment industry.

It turns out that McCarthy's original list was completely made up, and his political grandstanding ruined people's lives. President Eisenhower issued Executive Order 10450 on April 27, 1953, rescinding President Truman's executive order but making it illegal for LGBTQ2+ people to work in the civil service because of a perceived security risk. Because they were *perceived* to be LGBTQ2+, more than five thousand people were fired and had their personal lives exposed for all the world to see.

Where you store your data is a critically important part of the process. You must not put your people at risk simply because you didn't do your homework. And for most clients, Survey Monkey stores their data on servers in the United States.[5] Just sayin'.

Key Takeaways

- Asking your people about their sexual orientation and gender identity is important because it can tell you who your people are and how included they feel.

- There are specific strategies to respectfully ask questions about sexual orientation and gender identity and to encourage participation.

- Sex, gender, and sexual orientation are all different things, so you need to ask about each separately.

10

MARKETING TO LGBTQ2+ PEOPLE

It is absolutely
imperative that every
human being's freedom and
human rights are respected,
all over the world.

JÓHANNA SIGURÐARDÓTTIR, former Icelandic
prime minister and the first openly LGBTQ2+ head of state

Part of the bigger LGBTQ2+ conversation is about how to attract LGBTQ2+ people to your organization as a customer (or client or whatever word you use), and this is just as relevant when you are looking to attract volunteers, employees, students, and patients. It's important to understand how to market to LGBTQ2+ folks as potential employees and volunteers, but it's equally important to understand how to market to them as potential consumers. How can you get people like me to spend my hard-earned dollars on whatever it is you're selling? How can you get a piece of the infamous pink dollar?

To be clear, the dollar isn't actually pink. We're not going around changing the color of our money. It's a euphemism. I think. It might be an analogy. I'm pretty sure it's not a metaphor. Although the Cook Islands has a three-dollar bill that is pink. Sort of gives new meaning to the phrase "queer as a three-dollar bill." I am way off track.

Let me say one thing before I go on: I'm not a marketing professional. My knowledge and experience in marketing are quite significant, but there are people who have dedicated their lives to this. Some brilliant minds work in LGBTQ2+

specific marketing, and they could easily speak to this topic better than I can, but since they're not writing this book, I'm going to share with you some general ideas to consider when you're marketing to the LGBTQ2+ communities.

How Many Are There?

This is the magic number that everyone asks about. How many LGBTQ2+ people are there? To be clear, I'm super gay, but I don't know all of them.

There are conflicting reports. American researcher Alfred Kinsey released studies called *Sexual Behavior in the Human Male* (1948) and *Sexual Behavior in the Human Female* (1953) that indicated as many as 18 percent of men and 6 percent of women were pretty much exclusively homosexual.[1] It generally became accepted that approximately 10 percent of people were LGBTQ2+. From that research, Kinsey developed a scale (aptly named the Kinsey Scale), which was the first to measure sexuality on a spectrum.

Kinsey's research has subsequently been analyzed and reanalyzed, and a wide range of numbers have come out of it. The 10 percent rule has been proved and disproved. Additionally, subsequent studies have also produced an array of results. Frankly, it's hard to figure out which research report to believe.

It's generally accepted that the national number is somewhere between 6 and 8 percent, but it turns out that age is a mitigating factor. Consider that a recent study by Ipsos[2] found that 52 percent of Generation Z respondents (ages sixteen to twenty-two) identified as exclusively being attracted to the opposite sex. This is compared to 60 percent of millennials, 76 percent of Generation X, and 84 percent of baby boomers. That means that around fifty percent of young people identify as LGBTQ2+ in some way, compared to seven percent of the old farts. That doesn't mean that more of Gen Z than of Gen X or Y are LGBTQ2+. It suggests that (1) younger people are more comfortable identifying as such and don't feel the need to hide it; and/or (2) younger people are more willing and open as it relates to their sexuality and gender than older people, which is likely driven by societal acceptance.

It's all really confusing, I know. One thing researchers don't seem to consider is the social stigma attached to being LGBTQ2+. We still see many examples of homophobia, transphobia, and biphobia in day-to-day life, so people may be a little hesitant when a surveyor calls to ask who they have sex with. The United States and Canadian censuses now include a question about same-sex households, but it is entirely limiting, and it asks only if you're living with a person of the same sex in a romantic relationship. That excludes a lot of people who would identify as LGBTQ2+.

All of this is to say that, until such time as we have better data, it is a safe bet to assume that about 7 percent of the population identifies as LGBTQ2+.

The Value of the Pink Dollar

The pink dollar, sometimes called the "Dorothy dollar," which is a reference to Judy Garland's character from the *Wizard of Oz*, has been quantified by some, although the amounts are just estimates. If you didn't get the reference to the *Wizard of Oz*, you may want to spend some time genuflecting at Ms. Gardland's shrine and stop embarrassing yourself. This is a book about LGBTQ2+ inclusion, after all.

We don't have enough reliable data to know for sure. And when I say "reliable," I mean from organizations like the US Bureau of Statistics and Statistics Canada. This is my subtle way of publicly telling them to step up and start collecting data on LGBTQ2+ people.

That said, I believe the sources I'm quoting from are reliable enough to quote them. Globally, LGBT Capital estimates that the annual LGBT Gross Domestic Product (LGBT-GDP) is $3.6 trillion.[3] In the United States and Canada alone, the LGBT-GDP is estimated to be $1.086 trillion. That's trillion with a T, henny! Keep in mind that, according to the World Bank, the United States and Canada's GDP combined is $23.206 trillion, so LGBTQ2+ folks are responsible for an estimated 1.5 percent of the national GDP. And that, in my humble opinion, is a conservative estimate. In the United States, LGBT-GDP rivals other minority groups, such as African and Black Americans ($1.4 trillion GDP) and Hispanic and Latinx Americans ($1.7 trillion GDP), and Asian Americans ($1.2 trillion GDP).[4]

Let's think about that for a moment: There are around 60 million Hispanic and Latinx Americans; more than 40 million African and Black Americans; and around 23 million Asian Americans. If we assume that the LGBTQ2+ population makes up 7 percent of the US population, that's just shy of 23 million LGBTQ2+ Americans. Yet, that 23 million account for 1.1 trillion in the GDP. Let's put that in a chart just for clarity.

GROUP	POPULATION	GDP	GDP PER PERSON
Total	328 million	$20.94 trillion	$63,841.46
White Americans	235.4 million[5]	$13.2 trillion[6]	$56,074.77
African and Black Americans	40.6 million[7]	$1.4 trillion[8]	$34,482.76
Hispanic and Latinx Americans	60.6 million[9]	$1.7 trillion[10]	$28,052.81
Asian Americans	23.2 million[11]	$1.2 trillion[12]	$51,724.14
Native Americans	5.7 million[13]	$126.8 billion[14]	$22,245.61
Native Hawaiians	1.4 million[15]	Unknown	Unknown
LGBTQ2+ Americans	23 million	$1.1 trillion	$47,826.09

What we see is that LGBTQ2+ Americans are at a significantly higher GDP per person compared with almost all other minority groups. So, yeah, the pink dollar is valuable.

Why the LGBTQ2+ communities have so much more disposable dough can be attributed to a few factors, not the least of which is that a lot of LGBTQ2+ peeps fall into one of three categories: DINK (double income, no kids), DINKY (double income, no kids yet), or DINKWAD (double income, no kids, with a dog). Although a significant number of LGBTQ2+ folks have become parents over the past decade (since, you know, it's been legal for us to adopt), the majority of LGBTQ2+ people today do not have the burden and joy of children. I'm a perfect example, as I am sadly barren. My husband and I are classic DINKWADs (in so many ways). The consequence of that is we have more disposable income than people who are saving for their kid's college fund.

To be clear, this is a generalization. Just as with straight cisgender folks, lots of LGBTQ2+ people live well below the poverty line. Not all LGBTQ2+ people are driving around in luxury vehicles, buying million-dollar homes. But the numbers in the table above give you a sense of how much potential we're talking about.

Loyal to a Fault

The other piece of this puzzle is that LGBTQ2+ folks are loyal. Like, stupid loyal. According to a Harris Interactive study from 2007, 88 percent of LGBTQ2+ adults are likely to select a brand that is known to provide equal workplace benefits for all of their employees, including LGBTQ2+ people.[16] And there's more. So much more:

- When ordering alcohol, 60 percent of LGBTQ2+ people are more likely to ask for specific brands compared with 42 percent of heterosexual/cisgender people.[17]

- 71 percent of LGBTQ2+ people have pets, compared to 63 percent of straight cisgender people.[18]

- 55 percent of LGBTQ2+ consumers will choose to do business with companies that are committed to the diversity and equal treatment of the LGBTQ2+ communities.[19]

- 70 percent of LGBTQ2+ adults stated they would pay a premium for a product from a company that supports the LGBTQ2+ communities.[20]

- 78 percent of LGBTQ2+ adults and their friends and relatives would switch to brands that are known to be LGBTQ2+ friendly.[21]

So many numbers all to prove a point: LGBTQ2+ people tend to be loyal to the organizations that are loyal to them.

How to Do It Right

Now that you understand what's at stake, let's take a look at some things to consider when you decide you want to market to the LGBTQ2+ communities.

Advertising

Advertising is obviously a big part of marketing. For many organizations it's a huge part of their annual operating budget. Billions, if not trillions, of dollars are spent every year on advertising this, that, and the other thing. As part of advertising to LGBTQ2+ people, you should be looking at some important considerations:

LGBTQ2+ media. Do you advertise in LGBTQ2+ specific media? If your goal is to market to the LGBTQ2+ communities, connect with members of the communities where they already are.

There is a vast array of LGBTQ2+ specific media outlets, from the big ones—like *The Advocate*, *Out* magazine, OutTV, and Logo—to much smaller and more niche outlets that target specific groups. And don't forget about the social medias. We're big consumers of things like Instagram and Twitter.

You need to research which outlet attracts the people you're trying to reach, and then allot a certain piece of your budget to that outlet.

Mainstream media. LGBTQ2+ media is one thing—you know we're watching that. But mainstream media is also a place to advertise to LGBTQ2+ folks. We watch TV just like everyone else, and since 2019, Nielsen has been collecting data on what LGBTQ2+ people are watching. Did you know that the number one show for LGBTQ2+ folks is ... *The Connors*?[22] That's right. Post-Roseanne, my people tuned into *The Connors* in big numbers (no idea why—didn't like the show the first or second times around, so not watching it now), even though it rated thirty-first place overall.

Our radar is highly attuned, and we're paying attention to see if you are advertising to us in mainstream media. LGBTQ2+ messaging in mainstream media—where it can be seen by straight cisgender people—shows us that your commitment to LGBTQ2+ inclusion goes beyond pinkwashing. ("Pinkwashing" was originally used by Sarah Schulman in a piece for the *New York Times*.[23] The term suggests that certain actions intended to denote LGBTQ2+ inclusion are hiding a different reality, which is often quite contradictory. The Obama administration was accused of pinkwashing, according to Omar G. Encarnación, a professor of political studies at Bard College, "to distract from other unsavory policies such as the deportation of millions of undocumented immigrants and the failure to prosecute those responsible for the human rights abuses of the Bush administration's War on Terror."[24])

Your advertising doesn't have to be overt (no one actually wants to see a picture of people kissing; there's a name for that: porn). It can be subtle and quite effective. Amtrak's "Ride with Pride Campaign" from 2012, as an example, shows one ad with two African American women and a young African American girl, and one with two white men and a white boy. The headline reads: "Priceless family memories are now affordable."[25] I think it's safe to assume that these are supposed to be same-sex parents with their children. I see that and I get the message loud and clear.

Mainstream media advertising that uses LGBTQ2+ inclusive language and images sends a very powerful message about your position on LGBTQ2+ inclusion.

One size does not fit all. The LGBTQ2+ communities are as diverse as the entire world. It is not as simple as casting two white cis able-bodied men in your advertising and thinking that reflects all members of the communities. In fact, a lot of people would look at that image and find it offensive because it continues to perpetuate a stereotype.

If you must use images of people, make sure they are reflective of the broader population: people of color, women, Trans* and non-binary folks, people of diverse abilities, and so on. Using faces that look like the entire communities is critical. It's impossible for one image to include every identity within the communities, but you need to think about the images you do use to ensure you're not being exclusionary or stereotypical.

My advice is to altogether avoid using people in advertising and marketing. You are never going to achieve complete representation, and you risk alienating someone by the attempt. Better to find other ways to get your message across. But if you're really bent on using people, think it through.

To Pride or Not to Pride

I have mixed feelings about LGBTQ2+ pride as a marketing medium. I'm a big fan of pride, but I don't go to pride anymore. I know, I'm a bad gay.

I went to my first pride festival (no parade) in 1987, and over the course of my adult life I have been to literally hundreds of celebrations. In one year, I attended more than thirty pride festivals (it was in the job description: gay for pay), so I feel like I've done my part to celebrate. The hordes of people are too much for me, and I can just as easily sit in my backyard and celebrate, without paying twice as much for a drink that will be half as much the next day. Translation: I'm cheap and I hate crowds.

For people in my profession (as well as a lot of LGBTQ2+ folks working toward LGBTQ2+ inclusion while not getting paid for it), June is a rainbow marathon. It starts with a flag raising at City Hall on June 1, and it doesn't end until the last drop of cheap pinot grigio on the evening of June 30. Between then, I will have upward of three and four events every day. There are breakfast events, lunch events, and so, so, so many cocktail receptions. I love a glass of wine more than most, but honestly, it gets tiresome when you've been to your third pride party in one afternoon, seen many of the same people at each event, and they're all serving chardonnay (serving chardonnay should be a hate crime). There are speakers and panels and games and all sorts of fun. And keep in mind—this is the *lead-up* to pride weekend. Now take into consideration that pride festivals in the United States and Canada start as early as April and go as late as November. At some point, I'll need a new liver.

Marching in a pride parade is generally not a good marketing opportunity because pride parades have become so overly commercialized that people don't remember which float had which half naked person on it. Standing out is pretty much impossible.

Similarly, pride receptions are so common now. They're good for morale for your LGBTQ2+ employees and a symbol of your commitment to LGBTQ2+ inclusion, but not a good spend from a marketing perspective. The only way you can do it and attract attention is with a budget that rivals the GDP of some small countries.

I feel much the same way about having a booth at your local pride festival (assuming the event has some form of marketplace). It's of questionable value. Pride is a terrible place to recruit (what biases come into play when you see a potential candidate with electrical tape on their nipples?), and people do not go to a pride event to pick up a copy of whatever printed material you've created, as lovely as it may be.

If you want to go this route, be smart! Prepare a really creative and interactive experience. You have to figure out a way to engage with people who are often a little inebriated and not there actively seeking you out. How can you connect with people and somehow capture their information so you can engage with them when they don't have heatstroke? You might have a booth where you capture people's emails, and they spin a wheel for a chance to win a prize. The prize is not the point. The point is that you get their email addresses and reach out to them after pride weekend to recruit them as volunteers, donors, students, customers, and the like.

I'm not saying you shouldn't participate in pride, but consider how much you spend, and remember that I'm still going to be gay on July 1. Pinky swear. And, as I mentioned in chapter 5, you could celebrate several dates and not compete for space as intensely as you will during June. Here are a few to consider:

- International Transgender Day of Visibility, March 31

- Lesbian Visibility Day, April 26

- International Day Against Homophobia, Transphobia and Biphobia (IDAHOBIT), May 17

- Pansexual Visibility Day, May 24

- International Non-binary People's Day, July 14

- Celebrate Bisexuality Day, September 23

- National Coming Out Day, October 11

- International Pronouns Day, third Wednesday in October

- Intersex Awareness Day, October 26

- Transgender Day of Remembrance, November 20

Spread out the rainbow love. Look at some of the other amazing dates on the calendar and tie your marketing events to those celebrations.

Pinkwashing Your Logo

Pinkwashing your logo is what happens every June when thousands of organizations change their social media icons and websites to include a rainbow or other symbols to indicate their support for LGBTQ2+ inclusion. Every big organization does it, and lots of small ones do too. But my questions are: What is it going to look like on July 1? And is your commitment to LGBTQ2+ inclusion unwavering?

Regardless of the fact that you are going to offend some people by changing your logo to a rainbow version, you need to think beyond June. Pride is always a fantastic celebration of identity, but what happens in July, let alone December? Changing your logo doesn't erase the homophobia, transphobia, and biphobia that LGBTQ2+ folks face every day.

Where Your Money Meets Your Mouth

When I ask whether your commitment to LGBTQ2+ inclusion is unwavering, I am specifically referring to whether your actions match your words. The good and bad of the US system of politics and donations is that although corporations can donate to campaigns (they can't in Canada), that information is all publicly available. Oops.

According to the Center for Responsive Politics, in 2016, 2018, and the first quarter of 2020, seventeen company-affiliated Political Action Committees (PACs), all of which actively support the LGBTQ2+ communities through sponsorship of pride festivals or LGBTQ2+ advocacy organizations, gave more than $17 million dollars to representatives who oppose the Equality Act,[26] which "prohibits discrimination based on sex, sexual orientation, and gender identity in a wide variety of areas including public accommodations and facilities, education, federal funding, employment, housing, credit, and the jury system."[27]

I will refrain from listing all seventeen companies here or even singling out a few, not because I don't want to offend or embarrass them, but because it's not worth the ink. You can look it up for yourself. But the message I have for those seventeen companies, and for every organization, is that you cannot have it both ways. You don't get to be advocates of LGBTQ2+ inclusion and then donate to candidates who are actively working against that.

I know some people will say, "These donations are just business, and our company has an unwavering commitment to LGBTQ2+ inclusion. Just look at our HRC score." Blah freakin' blah! 🙄

And they will be right. They have the right to spend their money however they see fit. But I also have the right to spend my money how I see fit. There's no world in which I would ever support any of those seventeen companies, knowing they back candidates that have actively worked against my human rights.

Remember Target and their CEO Gregg Steinhafel? He said the exact same thing about his $150,000 donation, and that started a massive boycott that cost the company millions. Do you want that to happen to your organization?

Some employers will tell you they donate to candidates on both sides of the aisle, but two points in that pile of 💩 argument don't work. First, records show that corporate donations to Republicans far exceed those to Democrats; and second, you can't have it both ways. You can't play both shirts and skins because you're not sure who's going to win. One side is definitely going to lose. I'm fairly sure that's a sports reference. Or maybe I'm back to porn.

If you're an organization that has "values" or a corporate credo, you must decide how important those values are to you. Unwavering support means you draw a line in the sand and donate only to candidates who are aligned with those values.

Key Takeaways

- A general estimation is that 7 percent of the population is LGBTQ2+ identified.

- The pink dollar in the United States and Canada is worth more than $1 trillion dollars annually.

- Political donations reflect values, and if an organization values LGBTQ2+ inclusion, it should donate accordingly.

11

BEING AN ACTIVE ALLY

Why is it that, as a culture, we are **more comfortable** seeing two men holding guns than holding hands?

ERNEST J. GAINES, American author

W inston Churchill once said, "There is at least one thing worse than fighting with allies, and that is fighting without them." The circumstances may have been dramatically different, but the intention remains true. The LGBTQ2+ communities would not be where we are today without our allies—straight cisgender people—who have seen the terrible realities faced by LGBTQ2+ people and joined in the fight.

The word "ally" comes from the Latin word "*alligare*," meaning "to bind to."[1] In essence, it means to join forces; to align with a particular cause. But what does that mean for individuals?

The truth of the matter is that organizations can bend over backward to create inclusive spaces for LGBTQ2+ people—as employees, clients, students, volunteers, patients, and so on—but individuals make it or break it. If you're a total *phobe* (homo, trans, or bi), then it doesn't matter what the policy says or what the organization does—you possess your beliefs, and there's little anyone can do to change that.

To be an ally of the LGBTQ2+ communities means you align with the communities in opposition of homophobia, transphobia, and biphobia. You lend and leverage your privilege as a straight/cisgender person in support of LGBTQ2+ inclusion. In a workplace, that might look like publicly opposing oppressive treatment of LGBTQ2+ people in Brunei, as the UK's *Financial Times* did in 2019 by canceling an event at the Dorchester Hotel, which is owned by the sultan of Brunei.[2] In a congregation, it might look like supporting your openly LGBTQ2+ clergy, even if that is in opposition of Church doctrine, like the congregation of St. Bernadette Catholic Parish in Milwaukee, Wisconsin, did of Father Greg Greiten—one of the world's few openly gay priests.[3] In a hospital, that might look like doing outreach to the Trans* community to ensure that Trans* people are able to access the medical services they need, and that they're delivered by medical practitioners who are educated on those needs.

These are powerful acts and may go against conventional norms. But the power comes from the lack of self-interest. I can stand up and say we need to do more to create inclusive spaces for Trans* women of color, but I have an agenda in that I am a member of the LGTBQ2+ communities. The statement is even more powerful when it comes out of the mouth of a straight/cisgender person because, for all intents and purposes, they don't have as much skin in the game. That doesn't discount my position; it strengthens it.

Types of Allies

Some of you reading this book are what I would commonly refer to as the "choir" or the "converted." You have an

LGBTQ2+ child, parent, family member, friend, or coworker, and you believe in your heart that everyone deserves to be treated with dignity and respect regardless of their sexual orientation or gender identity and expression. I don't need to convince you. You didn't read this book to be convinced. You already believe.

So, you're an ally. But are you an *active* ally? I described the difference earlier in the book. (Please tell me you didn't skip to the end! The meaning of life is 42 and Rosebud was a sled.) In essence, the difference is that an armchair ally is passively supportive, and an active ally is actively supportive.

Most people don't know the difference between an armchair ally and an active ally. I appreciate allies however I get them, but truthfully, it's not enough to *not* be homophobic, transphobic, or biphobic. That's like saying you're pro-law and order, but you don't call the police when you see a crime committed. You're welcome to be passive—that's up to you. You're just not helping.

Consider this: You are at work and someone (usually the person who thinks they're the Jerry Lewis of their generation) decides to share a joke that may be mildly funny but makes an LGBTQ2+ person the punch line. The people around you seem amused, and none of them are LGBTQ2+ as far as you know. What do you do? How do you react?

The difference between an active ally and an armchair ally is in how they react. An armchair ally would think nothing of it. They would look around at who was present, and not seeing anyone they know to be LGBTQ2+, they would go on with their day without thinking about it. An active ally would take Chuckles the Clown aside and inform them that homophobic jokes are completely inappropriate and not to be told in your organization, or anywhere else for that matter. Whether there was an LGBTQ2+ person present to hear the joke is irrelevant. What if someone was closeted, or if they have an LGBTQ2+ family member? An active ally is more than willing to use their privilege (usually as a straight cis person) to ensure that the space is inclusive of LGBTQ2+ people, even when they're not in the room.

Hey, You, in the Back Row

You might think I want to speak to people who don't identify as allies. That's not correct. I consider some people to be a bit of a write-off. People who are actively homophobic, transphobic, or biphobic aren't going to read this book, so why would I bother committing any ink to them? No, that's not what this is about. This is the message for people who are sitting on the fence.

Some people reading this book might *think* they are big-A allies, but, politely, they are not. If you thought yourself an ally coming into this, how did you feel when you read the previous section? Which scenario best describes you? Are you actively involved? Are you listening? Are you learning? Are you as awesome as my mom?! (You are not as awesome as my mom, to be clear.)

The vast majority of people who *think* of themselves as allies are more armchair than active. Going to pride is not being an ally; it's enjoying a celebration. Watching *RuPaul's*

Drag Race does not an ally make—it makes someone with excellent taste in reality television programming. Allowing your LGBTQ2+ child to bring home their partner for Thanksgiving doesn't make you an ally; it makes you a human being with a soul.

I'm not here to judge. (Oh my goodness, I'm *sooo* here to judge.) If you're not an active ally, it doesn't mean you're a bad person. But it doesn't mean you are a good person either. It may seem a bit cruel, but I subscribe to the belief that if you're not part of the solution, you are part of the problem.

So maybe you're not the person who made the homophobic comment or told the transphobic joke. Maybe you're not the person who misgenders your non-binary colleague. Maybe you're not the person who asks your pansexual colleague why they "can't just pick one." Maybe not. But are you part of the solution? As a straight cisgender person you have a lot of power and privilege. You are part of the "majority." If I tell a person that their homophobic joke was offensive to me, it's very different than if my parents say something. I have an agenda. They don't.

To be completely clear, active allyship includes LGBTQ2+ folks, too, particularly those of us who are part of the "in crowd." As a white cisgender man, I have a ton of privilege that is not experienced by people of color, Trans* and non-binary folks, and many other members of the LGBTQ2+ communities. As such, I must use that privilege to be an ally to people of color, Trans* and non-binary folks, and the many other members of the LGBTQ2+ communities who need me to play that role. And I do it humbly and with pride.

What I'm trying to say is that it's time for you, as someone who identifies as an ally, to get up out of your armchair and get active!

Get Involved

So, you've decided you want to be an active ally, right? Mazel tov! Now you have to figure out what that means. Being an active ally is just that—it's an active role. But you may be asking, what does that look like? What are you going to do? What's your role in creating an inclusive society for LGBTQ2+ people? I'm so glad you asked.

First and foremost, being an active ally means to take action. Waving a rainbow flag at pride is not enough. You must commit to being an active ally and figure out what your role is. That involves things like not allowing homophobic, transphobic, or biphobic comments to stand when they're inevitably said around you. I'm not suggesting you throw on your *Xena: Warrior Princess* outfit and mercilessly beat the offender into submission. Take the person aside and make sure they understand how hurtful and inappropriate their words were. And at some point, we can discuss why you have that Xena outfit.

It also involves making sure LGBTQ2+ people have a seat at the table, and that whatever you're working on isn't inadvertently homophobic, transphobic, or biphobic. It involves applying an LGBTQ2+ lens to your work and being a voice if people don't feel comfortable or able to be that voice for themselves. Remember that homophobic/transphobic/biphobic joke I talked about a few pages ago? An active ally would say something to make it clear that kind of humor was inappropriate.

Close Mouth, Open Ears

Your job as an active ally is to listen. Don't speak on behalf of the LGBTQ2+ communities. You're a guest in our house—don't tell us what color to paint.

Listen for the purpose of learning and not for the purpose of solving, arguing, or justifying. When someone tells you they've experienced homophobic, transphobic, or biphobic behavior, your job is to listen and believe. Respectfully listening to LGBTQ2+ people and learning from their experiences can help you grow as an active ally.

I'm often reminded of a woman I knew many years ago in an organization we both volunteered with. Let's call her Bernadette because I can't for the life of me remember her name. Her son was gay, and she certainly would have described herself as an active ally. We were both part of a fundraising event that not only raised funds for this LGBTQ2+ organization but that also targeted the LGBTQ2+ community. Bernadette talked a lot and always had an opinion about how things should be done. She'd say things like, "Oh, the gays love gold, so we should decorate the venue in gold." She was sitting in a room of mostly LGBTQ2+ people, telling us what we like.

Bernadette didn't listen. She felt that it was her place to speak on other people's behalf. And not all gays love gold.

Lesson Time

To be an effective active ally, you have to be an educated ally. You must have at least a modicum of knowledge to understand what LGBTQ2+ people go through. Reading this book is a start because it provides good coverage of terminology, and there are some historical notes in here—but there is a lot more to learn.

Did you know the Stonewall riots—the events largely believed to have been the catalyst for what is now LGBTQ2+ inclusion—started because of severe police oppression, and the first stones were likely thrown by Black Trans* women? (There are varying stories on this one.) Before reading this book, did you know that being gay or lesbian is illegal in seventy-one countries? Did you know that up until recently men who had sex with men were required to be celibate in Canada and the United States before they could donate blood, because of stigma related to men who have sex with men and HIV/AIDS? This is changing as I type, but consider the impact of that message. In some countries it's as long as five years—if you're able to donate blood at all. Yeah, because if I haven't had sex for five years, the first thing I want to do is donate blood.

You need to know these things. You need to know not just what LGBTQ2+ people have faced in the past, but what we face today. Only then can you truly be engaged as an ally.

Once upon a time, a dear friend of mine, who is a Black woman, was complaining to me about how people touch her hair. I laughed because I thought it was a joke. She assured me that it wasn't and proceeded to explain how, when, and where countless people have randomly touched her hair without asking. I was stunned then and still am. But I couldn't know that information without having had it told to me. No one has ever tried to touch my hair. Mainly because there's not a lot of hair up there. And then I witnessed it ... and witnessed it ... and witnessed it. That lesson my friend taught me has meant that now when I witness someone touching a Black woman's hair, I call the person on it. Here endeth the lesson.

It's Not About You, Sweetie

This is one of those "not us without us" moments. Being an active ally does not mean you are a savior. That's not what is needed, Bernadette! We don't need a white knight to ride in on a stallion to save us. Unless we're working through a fantasy, but this is really not the time.

What is needed is for you to lend your voice and support to the cause; to yield to members of the communities; to advocate when it is required. Do not monopolize or patronize. Don't feel the need to be the leader. Be part of something bigger. If you're a straight cisgender professor at a college or university, you might become the faculty advisor of the LGBTQ2+ student group and advocate for that group with the leadership of the school. If you run a volunteer-based organization, you might consider putting together an LGBTQ2+

advisory group to become your sounding board on LGBTQ2+ inclusion in your organization's service delivery. In your workplace, you might support the initiatives of an LGBTQ2+ Employee Resource Group or advocate for LGBTQ2+ inclusion training for all employees.

There are lots of examples, but all you have to do is ask the question, "What can I do?" And then do it. That's what being an active ally is all about.

One of the best examples I have of what an active ally looks like was set by my mother, Karen. Before I get in trouble, my father is also a huge ally, but something in particular that my mom has done, and continues to do, is a perfect example of active allyship.

Karen Bach is an ordained member of the Presbyterian Church of Canada. She was ordained in 1990, and although she only had a "parish" for a hot minute, she played her part as campus chaplain at the University of Toronto for ten years, and then as the leader of a street youth mission for another fifteen.

Mom's allyship went well beyond being a good parent to a gay kid. At U of T she actively ensured that LGBTQ2+ students had a place of safety by always having her safe-space sticker on her office door. She was active in LGBTQ2+ activities on campus. She used her privilege as a straight white cisgender woman of the cloth to advocate for more inclusion on campus.

At Evergreen Centre for Street Youth, she continued her active ally work by changing policies to be more inclusive of LGBTQ2+ staff—in an organization that was started by the Baptist church. When she started, it wasn't the most LGBTQ2+ friendly place. (They actually had an employment contract that required employees to swear an oath that they were straight, but my mom made that go bye-bye.) What is most impressive to me is her work in the Church overall. She spent the past thirty years advocating—nay, fighting—to get the Presbyterian Church of Canada to ordain LGBTQ2+ clergy. And now they do.

She once told a mutual (gay) friend, "I know why God made Michael gay." My friend was terrified of what was about to come out of her mouth, but he pressed on. "Why?" he asked. "To put me on my path," she responded. She believes that is why God put her on the planet—to fight for LGBTQ2+ inclusion. #gogod

Key Takeaways

- Being an active ally is about getting involved and playing a role in something bigger.

- You need to educate yourself about what has happened and be aware of what is happening with LGBTQ2+ people.

- The best allies don't make it about themselves; they make it about LGBTQ2+ inclusion.

ACKNOWLEDGMENTS

Books like this don't happen overnight. There's a huge team of people who go into getting it from my keyboard to your hands. I want to thank the amazing team at Page Two for their love and support. They've taken me from a nervous little first-time author to a nervous little second-time author. At least I didn't have as many breakdowns this time.

I want to thank my family for being the fabulous, supportive people they are. If it weren't for their love and support, I wouldn't be the fabulous queen I am, writing this book.

There are so many amazing LGBTQ2+ people who have come before me and helped shape me—my chosen family. People like Marsha P. Johnson, the Trans* woman of color who threw the first brick during the Stonewall riots in New York City in 1969. I never had the privilege of meeting her, but I think we would've been fierce friends.

People like Reverend Brent Hawkes, who marched in Toronto's first pride protest after the bathhouse raids of February 5, 1981. Brent went on to lead the Metro Community

Church of Toronto and perform Canada's first same-sex marriage. He is one of the kindest people I have ever known.

People like Selisse Berry, who was the founding CEO of Out and Equal Workplace Advocates and who tirelessly fought for LGBTQ2+ workplace equality in the United States and around the world. Selisse and I have met on many occasions, and I have always been impressed by her vision.

People like Douglas Elliott, a lawyer who argued (and won) some of the most critical landmark cases in front of the Supreme Court of Canada related to LGBTQ2+ inclusion, including the case that led to marriage equality. I'm humbled by his intelligence and humility.

People like Jaime Watt, a political insider who manages to find a way to be a Conservative but at the same time fight for the rights of LGBTQ2+ people. I'm lucky to have him in my life.

People like my friend Jenn Finan, a queer Trans* woman who has overcome so much adversity and yet still remains one of the kindest souls I know. Jenn's story is littered throughout this book, but she also acted as one of my initial content editors to make sure I got it right.

And people like my other friend D.S. "Shep" Sheppard, a non-binary person who, while a relatively recent addition to my world, has become a dear and trusted friend and colleague. Shep also acted as one of my initial content editors, providing valuable insight as the voice of the/a non-binary person. I learn from them every day.

There are many more. Many, many more. I stand on the shoulders of giants, and all I can hope for is that I somehow do right by them.

Last but not least is my husband. He puts up with me when I work too hard; he keeps my feet on the ground when I want to fly away; he holds my hand when I'm sad. He never laughs at my jokes, because it's questionable if he has a sense of humor, but no one is perfect.

NOTES

Just so you don't think this book was all about my personal homosexual agenda, I include a list of all the materials that I referenced. 'Cause I'm smart and stuff. To make things easier for you to access these links, I have created an online repository of all the links below. You can find it at michaelbach.com. And, yes, I am that vain.

Opening Thoughts

1   "Violence Against the Transgender Community in 2019," Human Rights Campaign, hrc.org/resources/violence-against-the-transgender-community-in-2019.

Chapter 1: Making It about Me for a Change

Epigraph: Jason Collins, "Why NBA Center Jason Collins Is Coming Out Now," *Sports Illustrated*, April 29, 2013, si.com/ more-sports/2013/04/ 29/jason-collins-gay-nba-player.
1   Jack Drescher, "Out of DSM: Depathologizing Homosexuality," *Behavioral Sciences* 5, no. 4 (December 2015): 565–75, mdpi.com/ 2076-328X/5/4/565.
2   "Map of Countries that Criminalise LGBT People," Human Dignity Trust, humandignitytrust.org/lgbt-the-law/map-of-criminalisation.
3   "Map of Countries That Criminalise LGBT People."

4   "Map of Countries That Criminalise LGBT People."

5   Yvette Tan, "Brunei Implements Stoning to Death Under Anti-LGBT Laws," BBC News, April 3, 2019, bbc.com/news/world-asia-47769964.

6   "Brunei Says It Won't Enforce Death Penalty for Gay Sex," BBC News, May 6, 2019, bbc.com/news/world-asia-48171165.

7   Grace Hauck, "Anti-LGBT Hate Crimes Are Rising, the FBI Says. But It Gets Worse," *USA Today*, June 28, 2019, usatoday.com/story/news/2019/06/28/anti-gay-hate-crimes-rise-fbi-says-and-they-likely-undercount/1582614001.

8   Tim Fitzsimons, "Nearly 1 in 5 Hate Crimes Motivated by Anti-LGBTQ Bias, FBI Finds," NBC News, November 12, 2019, nbcnews.com/feature/nbc-out/nearly-1-5-hate-crimes-motivated-anti-lgbtq-bias-fbi-n1080891.

9   "Hate Crime Laws," Movement Advancement Project, lgbtmap.org/equality-maps/hate_crime_laws.

Chapter 2: Breaking Down the Alphabet

Epigraph: Zanele Muholi quoted in "20 Powerful LGBT Quotes That Made History," Human Rights Careers, humanrightscareers.com/issues/lgbt-quotes.

1   Sam Killermann, "Comprehensive* List of LGBTQ+ Vocabulary Definitions," It's Pronounced Metrosexual, itspronouncedmetrosexual.com/2013/01/a-comprehensive-list-of-lgbtq-term-definitions.

2   Sam Killermann, "Understanding the Complexities of Gender," TEDxUofIChicago, YouTube video, posted May 3, 2013, 16:28, itspronouncedmetrosexual.com/2013/05/my-ted-talk-understanding-the-complexities-of-gender.

3   *Will and Grace*, season 4, episode 16, "A Chorus Lie," directed by James Burrows, written by Tracy Poust and Jon Kinnally, aired February 7, 2002, on NBC.

4   "How Common Is Intersex?" Intersex Society of North America, isna.org/faq/frequency.

5   Jessica Murphy, "Toronto Professor Jordan Peterson Takes On Gender-Neutral Pronouns," BBC News, November 4, 2016, bbc.com/news/world-us-canada-37875695.

Chapter 3: Understanding Sexuality, Identity, and Expression

Epigraph: Tomson Highway, *Kiss of the Fur Queen* (Toronto: Anchor Canada, 1999).

1 Sam Killermann, "Comprehensive* List of LGBTQ+ Vocabulary Definitions," It's Pronounced Metrosexual, itspronouncedmetrosexual. com/2013/01/a-comprehensive-list-of-lgbtq-term-definitions.

Chapter 4: Straight and Cis until Proved Otherwise

Epigraph: Laverne Cox interviewed by bell hooks, "bell hooks: Transgressions," A Public Dialogue between bell hooks and Laverne Cox hosted by Eugene Lang College of Liberal Arts, YouTube video, posted October 13, 2014, 1:36:08, youtube.com/watch?v=9oMmZIJijgY.

1 Mahita Gajanan, "'Absolutely Not a Choice.' Elizabeth Smart's Father on Coming Out as Gay, Leaving Mormon Church," *Time*, December 10, 2019, time.com/5747294/elizabeth-smart-father-gay.

2 David Smith and Lucia Graves, "Supreme Court Sides with Baker Who Refused to Make Gay Wedding Cake," *Guardian*, June 4, 2018, theguardian.com/law/2018/jun/04/gay-cake-ruling-supreme-court-same-sex-wedding-colorado-baker-decision-latest.

3 Adapted from Martin Rochlin, "The Language of Sex: The Heterosexual Questionnaire," in *Privilege: A Reader*, 2nd ed., Michael S. Kimmel and Abby L. Ferber, eds. (Boulder: Westview Press, 2009), 95–97. See also higherlogicdownload.s3.amazonaws.com/NASN/e277e492-64b1-4f55-ac15-00857a7a5662/UploadedImages/Oregon%20Microsite/Documents/HeterosexualQuestionnaire.pdf.

Chapter 5: The Importance of Safe Space

Epigraph: Karl Heinrich Ulrichs quoted in "20 Powerful LGBT Quotes That Made History," Human Rights Careers, humanrightscareers.com/issues/lgbt-quotes.

1 Merriam-Webster, s.v. "safe space (*n.*)," merriam-webster.com/dictionary/safe%20space.

2 Moira Rachel Kenney, *Mapping Gay L.A.: The Intersection of Place and Politics* (Philadelphia: Temple University Press, 2001), 24.

3 Richard Dawkins (@RichardDawkins), Twitter, October 24, 2015, 4:49 p.m., twitter.com/RichardDawkins/status/658022567085801472.

4   *In and Out: Diverging Perspectives on LGBT Inclusion in the Workplace*
    (Toronto: Canadian Centre for Diversity and Inclusion, 2015), ccdi.ca/
    media/1070/20150528-report-lgbt-inclusion-in-the-workplace-en.pdf.

5   "Map of Countries that Criminalise LGBT People," Human Dignity
    Trust, humandignitytrust.org/lgbt-the-law/map-of-criminalisation.

6   "Map of Countries that Criminalise LGBT People."

7   "Map of Countries that Criminalise LGBT People."

8   Rick Braatz, "GLBT Community Honors Life of Murdered Seaman:
    Veterans Use Tragic Death as Rallying Cry against 'DADT,'" *Gay and
    Lesbian Times*, July 16, 2009, archived from the original on September
    26, 2011, web.archive.org/web/20110926122515/http://www.gay
    lesbiantimes.com/?id=15098.

9   Matt Pearce, "Transgender Woman Sentenced to Men's Prison in
    Minnesota Killing," *Los Angeles Times*, June 18, 2012, latimes.com/
    nation/la-xpm-2012-jun-18-la-na-nn-transgender-woman-sentenced-
    to-mens-prison-20120618-story.html.

10 "Scott Jones Says He Was Attacked for Being Gay," CBC News,
    December 11, 2013, cbc.ca/news/canada/nova-scotia/scott-jones-
    says-he-was-attacked-for-being-gay-1.2459289.

11 Alan Blinder, Frances Robles, and Richard Pérez-Peña, "Omar Mateen
    Posted to Facebook Amid Orlando Attack, Lawmaker Says," *New York
    Times*, June 16, 2016, nytimes.com/2016/06/17/us/orlando-shooting.
    html.

12 Lane Sainty, "'This Is Why We Need to Defend Safe Schools': LGBTI
    Community Responds to Gay Teen's Suicide," BuzzFeed, November 24,
    2016, buzzfeed.com/lanesainty/bullied-gay-teens-suicide-not-an-
    isolated-incident.

13 "London Bus Attack: Arrests after Gay Couple Who Refused to Kiss
    Beaten," BBC News, June 7, 2019, bbc.com/news/uk-england-london-
    48555889.

14 John Riley, "Three Men Arrested after Gay Couple Attacked for Holding
    Hands in Public," Metro Weekly, September 8, 2020, metroweekly.
    com/2020/09/three-men-in-canada-charged-with-assaulting-gay-man-
    for-holding-hands-with-another/.

15 Jamie Wareham, "Murdered, Suffocated and Burned Alive—350
    Transgender People Killed in 2020," Forbes, November 11, 2020, forbes.
    com/sites/jamiewareham/2020/11/11/350-transgender-people-have-
    been-murdered-in-2020-transgender-day-of-remembrance-list.

16 *Achieving and Sustaining Employment Equity: A Five-Step Process* (Human
    Resources and Skills Development Canada, 2012), equity.esdc.gc.ca/
    docs/Step2-2EN.pdf.

17 "Whatever It Takes to Ensure Equality for All Kids," Boys and Girls
     Clubs of America, bgca.org/programs/initiatives/LGBTQ-Initiative.
18 Sue Sneyd, "Being Ourselves at Work," *Canadian Government Executive*,
     May 7, 2012, canadiangovernmentexecutive.ca/being-ourselves-at-work.
19 Lindsay Sears, *2017 Retention Report: Trends, Reasons & Recommenda-
     tions* (Franklin, TN: Work Institute, August 2017), info.workinstitute.
     com/retentionreport2017.
20 Christina Merhar, "Employee Retention: The Real Cost of Losing an
     Employee," People Keep, June 2, 2020, peoplekeep.com/blog/bid/
     312123/employee-retention-the-real-cost-of-losing-an-employee.
21 Matt Mullen, "The Pink Triangle: From Nazi Label to Symbol of Gay
     Pride," History, history.com/news/pink-triangle-nazi-concentration-
     camps.
22 W. Jake Newsome, "Pink Triangle Legacies: Holocaust Memory and
     International Gay Rights Activism," Nursing Clio, April 20, 2017,
     nursingclio.org/2017/04/20/pink-triangle-legacies-holocaust-memory-
     and-international-gay-rights-activism/#footnoteref2.
23 Nora Gonzalez, "How Did the Rainbow Flag Become a Symbol of
     LGBTQ Pride?," Brittanica, britannica.com/story/how-did-the-
     rainbow-flag-become-a-symbol-of-lgbt-pride.
24 Jamie Wareham, "Why Many LGBT People Have Started Using a New
     Pride Flag," Forbes, July 12, 2020, forbes.com/sites/jamiewareham/
     2020/07/12/why-lgbt-people-have-started-using-a-new-pride-flag-
     nhs-black-lives-matters.

Chapter 6: The Case for Inclusive Organizations

Epigraph: Christine Jorgensen quoted in "20 Powerful LGBT Quotes That
     Made History," Human Rights Careers, humanrightscareers.com/
     issues/lgbt-quotes.
1   John Martin, "This Year's Rent...," *A Day in the Life: Digital Digressions*,
     Live Journal, Daily Affirmation, February 16, 2012, dailyafirmation.
     livejournal.com/1001695.html.
2   John Martin LinkedIn message to Michael Bach, July 16, 2020.
3   "The Average Canadian Salaries by Industry and Region," Workopolis,
     December 22, 2017, careers.workopolis.com/advice/how-much-money-
     are-we-earning-the-average-canadian-wages-right-now.
4   Steve Fiorillo, "The Average Income in the U.S.," The Street, thestreet.
     com/personal-finance/average-income-in-us-14852178.

5   Frank Newport, "In U.S., Estimate of LGBT Population Rises to 4.5%,"
    Gallup, May 22, 2018, news.gallup.com/poll/234863/estimate-lgbt-
    population-rises.aspx.

6   The World Bank, data.worldbank.org/indicator/SL.TLF.TOTL.IN?
    locations=CA.

7   The World Bank, data.worldbank.org/indicator/SL.TLF.TOTL.IN?
    locations=us.

8   Sylvia Ann Hewlett and Karen Sumberg, "For LGBT Workers, Being
    'Out' Brings Advantages," *Harvard Business Review*, July–August 2011, hbr.
    org/2011/07/for-lgbt-workers-being-out-brings-advantages.

9   David Hudson, "Salvation Army Commander: Yes, We Are Faith-Based
    Charity. But We Serve and Love Everyone," *USA Today*, November 22,
    2019, usatoday.com/story/opinion/voices/2019/11/22/salvation-army-
    lgbt-backlash-poverty-gay-marriage-column/4269694002.

10 Zack Ford, "Salvation Army among New York City Drug Clinics
    Rejecting Transgender People," Think Progress, July 19, 2017, think
    progress.org/transgender-substance-abuse-discrimination-salvation-
    army-6470b6abc397.

11 Gaby Del Valle, "The Salvation Army Says It Doesn't Discriminate
    Against LGBTQ People. Critics Say That's Not True," Vox, December 16,
    2019, vox.com/the-goods/2019/12/16/21003560/salvation-army-anti-
    lgbtq-controversies-donations.

12 M.V. Lee Badgett, Laura E. Durso, Christy Mallory, and Angeliki Kastanis,
    The Business Impact of LGBT-Supportive Workplace Policies (Los Angeles:
    The Williams Institute, 2013), escholarship.org/uc/item/3vt6t9zx.

Chapter 7: Attracting LGBTQ2+ People

Epigraph: Barbara Gittings quoted in "20 Powerful LGBT Quotes That
    Made History," Human Rights Careers, humanrightscareers.com/
    issues/lgbt-quotes.

1   "Lexmark Earns Perfect Score for LGBTQ Workplace Equality for 13th
    Time," Lexmark Blog, April 10, 2019, lexmark.com/en_us/lexmark-
    blog/2019/lexmark-earns-perfect-score.html.

2   "BCG's Commitment to Diversity, Equity, and Inclusion," Boston Con-
    sulting Group, bcg.com/capabilities/diversity-inclusion/commitments.

3   Wesley Whistle, "What Does Today's LGBT Supreme Court Ruling
    Mean for Schools?" Forbes, June 15, 2020, forbes.com/sites/wesley
    whistle/2020/06/15/what-does-todays-lgbt-supreme-court-ruling-
    mean-for-schools/#5cc36eca7455.

4   Kieran Blake, "'A Political Fight Over Beer': The 1977 Coors Beer Boycott, and the Relationship Between Labour–Gay Alliances and LGBT Social Mobility," Midlands Historical Review [now The MHR], January 24, 2020, midlandshistoricalreview.com/a-political-fight-over-beer-the-1977-coors-beer-boycott-and-the-relationship-between-labour-gay-alliances-and-lgbt-social-mobility/#_ftn6.

5   "Target Homophobia? CEO Gregg Steinhafel Defends $150K Donation to Anti-Gay Politician, LGBT Community Angered," HuffPost, July 27, 2010, huffpost.com/entry/target-homophobia-ceo-gre_n_660990.

6   "Target Homophobia."

7   Natalie Hope McDonald, "Target Continued Anti-Gay Donations," Philadelphia magazine, December 22, 2010, phillymag.com/news/2010/12/22/target-continued-anti-gay-donations.

8   "Gaga Dissolves Deal with Target," Advocate, March 8, 2011, advocate.com/arts-entertainment/entertainment-news/2011/03/08/gaga-dissolves-deal-target.

Chapter 8: Retaining LGBTQ2+ People

Epigraph: Harvey Milk quoted in "20 Powerful LGBT Quotes That Made History," Human Rights Careers, humanrightscareers.com/issues/lgbt-quotes.

1   The 5 Fs Continuum from "Leading with Passion and Courage," Johnston Smith International, 2002.

2   Michael Bach, Birds of All Feathers: Doing Diversity and Inclusion Right (Vancouver: Page Two, 2020), 79.

3   Charles Duncan, "Dozens of States Consider Laws Banning Transgender Women from Team Sports," Spectrum News, NY1, March 29, 2021, ny1.com/nyc/all-boroughs/politics/2021/03/29/dozens-of-states-consider-laws-banning-transgender-women-from-team-sports.

4   "Heroes of Employee Engagement: No. 9 William Kahn," Peakon Post, May 3, 2018, peakon.com/us/blog/employee-success/william-kahn-employee-engagement.

5   "Actions speak louder than words," The Phrase Finder, phrases.org.uk/meanings/actions-speak-louder-than-words.html.

6   Brianna Whiting, "Zero-Tolerance Policy in the Workplace: Definition and Examples," Study.com, study.com/academy/lesson/zero-tolerance-policy-in-the-workplace-definition-examples-quiz.html.

7   Mary P. Rowe and Anna Giraldo-Kerr, "Gender Microinequities," *The SAGE Encyclopedia of Psychology and Gender*, July 27, 2017, mitsloan.mit. edu/shared/ods/documents/?DocumentID=4275.

8   Elizabeth Hopper, "What Is a Microaggression? Everyday Insults with Harmful Effects," ThoughtCo., July 3, 2019, thoughtco.com/micro aggression-definition-examples-4171853.

9   Simon Hattenstone, "The Dad Who Gave Birth: 'Being Pregnant Doesn't Change Me Being a Trans Man,'" *Guardian*, April 20, 2019, theguardian .com/society/2019/apr/20/the-dad-who-gave-birth-pregnant-trans-freddy-mcconnell.

10   *Template for Gender Transition Guidelines* (Washington, DC: Human Rights Campaign Foundation, 2015), assets2.hrc.org/files/images/ general/Module_4x_Gender_Transition_Guidelines_Template.pdf.

11   Alison Grenier and Jacq Hixson-Vulpe, *Beyond Diversity: An LGBT Best Practice Guide for Employers* (Toronto: Great Place to Work and Pride at Work Canada, 2017), prideatwork.ca/wp-content/uploads/2017/09/ Beyond-Diversity-LGBT-Guide.pdf.

12   Dictionary.com, s.v. "picture is worth a thousand words, one," dictionary. com/browse/picture-is-worth-a-thousand-words--one.

13   Stephanie Lottridge, "8 of the Best LGBT-Friendly Ads," Hearst Bay Area, June 7, 2017, marketing.sfgate.com/blog/8-of-the-best-lgbt-friendly-ads.

14   "LGBTQ Executive Leadership Program," Stanford Graduate School of Business, gsb.stanford.edu/exec-ed/programs/lgbtq-executive-leadership-program.

15   Olivia Schaber, "Exclusive: Inside the LGBTQ Executive Leadership Program at Stanford," *Silicon Valley Business Journal*, August 8, 2017, bizjournals.com/sanjose/news/2017/08/08/exclusive-inside-the-lgbtq-executive-leadership.html.

Chapter 9: You Measure What You Treasure

Epigraph: Troy Perry quoted in "20 Powerful LGBT Quotes That Made History," Human Rights Career, humanrightscareers.com/issues/ lgbt-quotes.

1   john a. powell and Stephen Menendian, "The Problem of Othering: Towards Inclusiveness and Belonging," Othering and Belonging, otheringandbelonging.org/the-problem-of-othering.

2   Russell Goldman, "Here's a List of 58 Gender Options for Facebook Users," ABC News, February 13, 2014, abcnews.go.com/blogs/head-lines/2014/02/heres-a-list-of-58-gender-options-for-facebook-users.

3   "Who, What, Where, When, Why," The LGBT Purge, lgbtpurge.com/
    about-lgbt-purge.

4   Robert Justin Goldstein, "Prelude to McCarthyism: The Making of a
    Blacklist," *Prologue* 38, no. 3 (Fall 2006): archives.gov/publications/
    prologue/2006/fall/agloso.html.

5   "Data Processing Agreements, Storage, and Transfers," Survey Monkey,
    help.surveymonkey.com/articles/en_US/kb/SurveyMonkey-Data-
    Transfers-and-EU-Laws.

Chapter 10: Marketing to LGBTQ2+ People

Epigraph: Jóhanna Sigurðardóttir quoted in "20 Powerful LGBT Quotes
    That Made History," Human Rights Careers, humanrightscareers.com/
    issues/lgbt-quotes.

1   "Diversity of Sexual Orientation," Kinsey Institute, kinseyinstitute
    .org/research/publications/historical-report-diversity-of-sexual-
    orientation.php.

2   Sara Machi and Chris Jackson, "Gender Identity and Sexual Orientation
    Differences by Generation," *Ipsos*, February 23, 2021, ipsos.com/en-us/
    gender-identity-and-sexual-orientation-differences-generation.

3   "Estimated LGBT Purchasing Power: LGBT-GDP—2018," LGBT
    Capital, lgbt-capital.com/docs/Estimated_LGBT-GDP_(table)_-_
    2018.pdf.

4   Jeff Green, "LGBT Purchasing Power Near $1 Trillion Rivals Other
    Minorities," Bloomberg, July 20, 2016, bloomberg.com/news/articles/
    2016-07-20/lgbt-purchasing-power-near-1-trillion-rivals-other-
    minorities.

5   ACS Demographic and Housing Estimates, United States
    Census Bureau, data.census.gov/cedsci/table?d=ACS%20
    5-Year%20Estimates%20Data%20Profiles&tid=ACSDP5Y2019.
    DP05&hidePreview=true.

6   "Buying Power," Catalyst, April 27, 2020, catalyst.org/research/
    buying-power.

7   Profile: Black/African Americans, US Department of Health and Human
    Services, Office of Minority Health, minorityhealth.hhs.gov/omh/
    browse.aspx?lvl=3&lvlid=61.

8   "Buying Power."

9   Luis Noe-Bustamante, Mark Hugo Lopez, and Jens Manuel Krogstad,
    "U.S. Hispanic Population Surpassed 60 Million in 2019, but Growth
    Has Slowed," Pew Research Center, July 7, 2020, pewresearch.org/

fact-tank/2020/07/07/u-s-hispanic-population-surpassed-60-million-in-2019-but-growth-has-slowed.

10 "Buying Power."

11 Abby Budiman and Neil G. Ruiz, "Key Facts about Asian Americans, a Diverse and Growing Population," April 29, 2021, Pew Research Center, pewresearch.org/fact-tank/2021/04/29/key-facts-about-asian-americans.

12 "Buying Power."

13 Profile: American Indian/Alaska Native, US Department of Health and Human Services, Office of Minority Health, minorityhealth.hhs.gov/omh/browse.aspx?lvl=3&lvlid=62.

14 "Buying Power."

15 Profile: Native Hawaiians/Pacific Islanders, US Department of Health and Human Services, Office of Minority Health, minorityhealth.hhs.gov/omh/browse.aspx?lvl=3&lvlid=65.

16 *The Lesbian, Gay, Bisexual and Transgender (LGBT) Population At-A-Glance* (Harris Interactive/Witeck-Combs Communications, 2010), witeck.com/wp-content/uploads/2013/03/HI_LGBT_SHEET_WCC_AtAGlance.pdf.

17 *Lesbian, Gay, Bisexual and Transgender (LGBT) Population.*

18 *Lesbian, Gay, Bisexual and Transgender (LGBT) Population.*

19 Jenn Grace, "Why Is Brand Loyalty So Important in the LGBT Community?" Medium, January 6, 2017, medium.com/@JennTGrace/why-is-brand-loyalty-so-important-in-the-lgbt-community-357b8a9d115.

20 Grace.

21 Grace.

22 John Koblin, "L.G.B.T. Households Are Now Nielsen Families, and Advertisers and Producers Get a Valuable Tool," *New York Times*, May 1, 2019, nytimes.com/2019/05/01/business/media/nielsen-lgbtq-household-ratings.html.

23 Sarah Schulman, "Israel and 'Pinkwashing,'" *New York Times*, November 22, 2011, nytimes.com/2011/11/23/opinion/pinkwashing-and-israels-use-of-gays-as-a-messaging-tool.html.

24 Omar G. Encarnación, "Trump and Gay Rights: The Future of the Global Movement," *Foreign Affairs*, February 13, 2017, foreignaffairs.com/articles/2017-02-13/trump-and-gay-rights.

25 Alexandra Temblador, "LGBT Advertisements Are Becoming More Mainstream," The Next Family, February 19, 2015, thenextfamily.com/2015/02/companies-that-embrace-lgbt-families-in-advertising.

26 Reid Champlin, "Companies' Political Spending Contradicts Pride
    Support," OpenSecret News, June 13, 2019, opensecrets.org/news/
    2019/06/companies-political-spending-contradicts-pride-support.
27 H.R.5—Equality Act, Congress.gov, congress.gov/bill/116th-congress/
    house-bill/5.

Chapter 11: Being an Active Ally

Epigraph: Ernest J. Gaines quoted in Jeremy Goldman, "Celebrating Pride:
    17 Powerful LGBT Quotes," Inc., inc.com/jeremy-goldman/celebrating-
    pride-17-powerful-lgbt-quotes.html.
1 Vocabulary.com, s.v. "ally," vocabulary.com/dictionary/ally.
2 Emily Dixon, "More Companies Boycott Brunei over Anti-gay Laws,"
    CNN, April 5, 2019, cnn.com/2019/04/05/asia/brunei-hotel-airline-
    boycott-scli-intl.
3 Sari Aviv and Anna Matranga, "Gay Priests: Breaking the Silence,"
    CBS News, March 28, 2021, cbsnews.com/news/gay-priests-breaking-
    the-silence.

READING GUIDE

1   Some readers have described *Alphabet Soup* as "mind-bending" and "eye-opening." What did you learn that surprised you?

2   You've read Michael Bach's first book, *Birds of All Feathers*, right? Given everything you have learned about diversity and inclusion so far, why do you think a deep dive into LGBTQ2+ inclusion, specifically, is important?

3   In chapter 1, you read that, at the time of writing, being gay and lesbian is illegal in seventy-one countries worldwide, and that in North America, thousands of LGBTQ2+ people experience hate crimes each year. Knowing this, what do you think it might be like for an LGBTQ2+ person to make seemingly simple choices such as where to go on vacation, which businesses to frequent, and with whom to share the name of their spouse?

4   What is the difference between sex and gender? What about between gender identity and sexual orientation?

5   What are the definitions of each of these terms: "Trans*," "cisgender," "agender," and "genderqueer"? Refer back to pages 33-37 for a refresher if you are unsure of their

meanings. Which of the differences between these words are new to you?

6 Since reading *Alphabet Soup,* have you noticed any discrepancies between the way people use the terms "male" and "female" or "men" and "women" and how these terms are defined in the book? For example, read the following quote from the insightful article "Who Lost the Sex Wars" by Amia Srinivasan in *The New Yorker* (September 13, 2021), and determine what might be wrong with what the author is saying: "Trans advocates typically distinguish between gender identity (whether people feel themselves to be male or female or something else) and gender expression (how "feminine" or "masculine" they self-present)."

7 Consider this scenario: When Gemma was born, the doctor yelled, "It's a girl!" And this lovely youngster spent most of her early life identifying as female. In high school, she had an inkling that she was primarily attracted to girls, but it wasn't until college that Gemma came out as a lesbian. Years later, in July 2005, after same-sex marriage was legalized in Canada, she married Molly, her long-time partner. Then, in her early thirties, Gemma noticed she had begun feeling attracted to men, and gay men specifically. She slowly came to realize, though, that she was not bisexual—rather, *they* were bigender. After adopting the pronoun "they" and changing their name to Gem, they came out a second time. What do you think about Gem's experience? How do you relate? What do you think it's like to live through that experience?

8 If you haven't already, answer the Heterosexual Questionnaire on page 67. How did it make you feel? What did it
make you think about? How will you act if/when you hear
similar questions asked of LGBTQ2+ people?

9 Truth time: Have you ever found yourself presuming a
person's spouse is the "opposite" gender? What about
tacitly assuming that a friend's child, your customers, or
certain public figures are straight? When you find out a
person is LGBTQ2+, have you ever thought, "Hmmm,
you don't look gay"? Do you ask new acquaintances
what pronouns they use, and if so, in what circumstances?
(There's no judgment here—this is all about raising
awareness.) What are some benefits of unpacking heteronormative and cisnormative ways of thinking and being?

10 Before reading this book, in what context did you encounter the term "safe space"? Why do you think creating safe
space is so important in relation to LGBTQ2+ inclusion?
In what ways can you create safe space?

11 Organizational policies and procedures need to be inclusive to create safe space. Has your organization conducted
an employee systems review (ESR) to identify the barriers
to LGBTQ2+ inclusion? If not, why? If it has, what areas
need the most attention and what are you doing to address
the problems?

12 Even if you do not have an ESR to refer to, in which
areas do you imagine your organization could improve
LGBTQ2+ inclusion? (For example, is parental leave
extended to LGBTQ2+ people? Do training or orientation materials use inclusive language that accounts for
more than binary genders of man and woman, and do

they mention sexual orientation or gender identity and expression specifically?) What can your organization do to be more LGBTQ2+ inclusive?

13 Consider this scenario: Ted is a top salesperson who has been at the company for more than two decades. He gets along well with almost everyone and is much-loved by his peers. The other day, at a department meeting, he made an offhand joke at the expense of Trans* people. He didn't sound like he meant to be hurtful, and has no prior record of being Trans*phobic, biphobic, or homophobic. There are no LGBTQ2+ people at the company. What would you do if you were Ted's colleague? What would you do if you were Ted's boss?

14 Think about when you have felt the need to conceal something about yourself at work, at school, or even in a social situation, perhaps about your politics or your favorite extracurricular activity (LARPers unite!)? How is hiding one's LGBTQ2+ identity different from those examples?

15 Revisit "Will and Ned's Excellent Adventure" on page 103. What can you do at work (or school or church or in your community) to improve situations where colleagues may feel they have to hide their identities?

16 Name three or four organizations you have seen appealing to the LGBTQ2+ communities through their marketing and branding. How are they doing this? Now, think of your organization's internal and external communications materials. How are they reaching LGBTQ2+ audiences? What's effective about them, and what could work better?

17 What sorts of rewards and benefits does your organization specifically tailor to its LGBTQ2+ employees? How can they be improved to better retain LGBTQ2+ people?

18 What is your understanding of the role of an active ally versus an armchair ally? How would you define yourself? If you are not an active ally now, do you feel ready to take on the role? What might that look like for you, at home, at work, or in your community?

19 Here's another scenario: Sydney likes to go for drinks with their colleagues after work, but it's been less enjoyable lately. Ever since Wanda, who recently transferred divisions, started joining them, she's been making a point of sitting near Sydney. After a glass of wine or two, Wanda loudly announces that because her best friend, Lisa, is a lesbian, she knows all about being an LGBTQ2+ ally. Wanda has a habit of "slipping up," referring to Sydney as "he," and giggling about it, saying, "Oops, *sooorrry*. Lisa always gets mad at me when I do that." No one else at the table responds. Soon, Sydney stops attending happy hour. What issues might be at play here? How might Wanda's behavior impact Sydney? What might you do if you were at that table?

20 Consider various organizations and communities you are part of (your work, congregation, yoga studio, volunteer role, or school). How LGBTQ2+ inclusive are they? What is one concrete step you could take to make an organization you are affiliated with more LGBTQ2+ inclusive?

ABOUT THE AUTHOR

Michael Bach is the CEO of CCDI Consulting. He is nationally and internationally recognized as a thought leader and subject matter expert in the fields of inclusion, diversity, equity, and accessibility, bringing a vast knowledge of leading practices in a live setting to his work.

Michael has a post-graduate certificate in Diversity Management from Cornell University and holds the Cornell Certified Diversity Professional, Advanced Practitioner (CCDP/AP) designation.

His 2020 book, *Birds of All Feathers: Doing Diversity and Inclusion Right*, is a *Globe and Mail*, *Toronto Star*, and Amazon best-seller, and recipient of the silver 2020 Nautilus Book Award in the category of Rising to the Moment. Michael lives in Toronto, Canada, with his husband and their two Siberian huskies, Sasha and Pepper.